INTIMACY
with
GOD

CHRISTIAN DISCIPLINES
for SPIRITUAL GROWTH

INTIMACY

with

GOD

CHRISTIAN DISCIPLINES
for SPIRITUAL GROWTH

JOHN CALDWELL, D. MIN.

To Jan, Shan, and Jennifer,
for their support and sacrifice throughout the years;
and to Mary for her invaluable assistance
in preparing this manuscript

Table of Contents

Introduction

It is my conviction that much of the weakness of the modern-day church can be attributed to the lack of a strong, personal devotional life among most Christians in general and many Christian leaders in particular. That conviction prompted me to do the research which in turn motivated the sermon series which is the basis for this book.

There has been a growing awareness on my part that personal spiritual growth is directly related to a Christian's individual devotional life and the practice of Christian disciplines. My own spiritual growth has been most significant when I have really been into the Word, spending time alone with the Lord in prayer and meditation, and worshiping Him in my own quiet time. Several years ago, I read Richard Foster's *Celebration of Discipline* which was a tremendous encouragement to me in this area. It enhanced an ever increasing hunger for personal spiritual growth in my life although progress in the practice of the disciplines was slow in coming.

I knew how weak I was in the practice of spiritual disciplines, but I suspected that what was true of me was also true of a broad spectrum of Christians. My suspicions were confirmed by three surveys.

First, I wrote to sixty-five prominent Christian leaders in seventeen different states. These were pastors of large churches, Bible college professors, administrators, editors, and agency directors. Each was asked to make bibliographical recommendations in regard to the disciplines, provide helpful suggestions from their personal practice, and make observations concerning the state of the church in regard to the practice of spiritual disciplines.

Next, a survey was taken of 105 Indianapolis area ministers in regard to their personal practice of the disciplines. An astonishing eighty-eight of the 105 surveyed (84 per cent) responded.

The third and final preliminary survey was to be the most directly relevant in preparing the series of messages which was to follow. This was the survey of the members of Kingsway, my own congregation. The complete results of the second and third surveys are found in the appendices of this book. However, suffice it to say that while the results were not surprising, they were disappointing. I am especially indebted to over 500 members of the Kingsway congregation who participated in the survey. To their credit, I must say that they were very receptive to the emphasis on spiritual disciplines which followed; an emphasis which included a ten-part sermon series, homework assignments, reading, and personal accountability. They were not only receptive and affirming of the emphasis; but also responsive as the survey taken following the emphasis indicated (again, see the appendices). This final survey demonstrated significant improvement in the practice of every Christian discipline covered. It would appear that Christians are desirous of spiritual growth and are open to the practice of spiritual disciplines when taught and challenged.

On a very personal level, this study has also been a success. I certainly have not arrived. However, I am far more consistent in my devotional life than ever before. I am spending more time in prayer and personal Bible study than ever, and I am deriving greater benefit from it. Meditation is now a meaningful part of my devotional experience, and I am genuinely learning what it means to worship the Lord. I still struggle with consistency in keeping my journal, but I have made considerable progress. Fasting is an important part of my spiritual life, but unfortunately, all too often the flesh wins out over the spirit. The discipline of confession is an important part of my prayer life and has led to some restored interpersonal relationships as well. Furthermore, I am learning to see my ministry, my service to others, as a devotional exercise in itself. God has used the accountability I feel toward the people to whom I preach as a powerful reinforcement for the practice of the disciplines in my own life.

In the modern-day church heavy in its emphasis on programming, methods, and activity, the very basis of Christian life and experience, the inner life, has been sadly neglected. Outward conformity has become the level of expectation rather than genuine spirituality. There is a desperate need for spiritual renewal in the church. A renewed emphasis on spiritual disciplines can play an important part as long as it does not fall into the trap of being just another form of legalistic conformity.

Let me add one other tremendously important warning. It is imperative in our efforts to grow deeper spiritually that we not become so introspective that we fail to carry out Christ's mandate evangelistically and socially. Monasticism and asceticism are not the answer. However, there must be a balance in the Christian life. Otherwise, we will be busy doing things that have no lasting substance; or we will be heavenly minded but of no earthly use. The search for that balance is an ongoing one, and its goal a difficult one to attain! However, my prayer for this book is that it will be of help and encouragement to my fellow pilgrims in achieving that balance.

John Caldwell
October, 1992

Chapter One

BORN TO GROW

You have been born again not of seed which is perishable but imperishable, that is, through the living and abiding word of God (I Pet. 1:23).

Therefore, putting aside all malice and all guile and hypocrisy and envy and all slander, like newborn babes, long for the pure milk of the word, that by it you may grow in respect to salvation, if you have tasted the kindness of the Lord (I Pet. 2:1-3).

But grow in the grace and knowledge of our Lord and Savior Jesus Christ (II Pet. 3:18).

Just as the physical man is to grow physically after his physical birth, so Peter makes it clear that the spiritual man is to grow following the new birth. That's normal. That's natural. Lack of growth is abnormal and unnatural.

Furthermore, what is true of the individual Christian is to be true corporately of the church, the body of Christ.

> And He gave some as apostles, and some as prophets, and some as evangelists, and some as pastors and teachers, for the equipping of the saints for the work of service, to the building up of the body of Christ; until we all attain to the unity of the faith, and of the knowledge of the Son of God, to a mature man, to the measure of the stature which belongs to the fullness of Christ. As a result, we are no longer to be children tossed here and there by waves and carried about by every wind of doctrine, by the trickery of men, by craftiness in deceitful scheming; but speaking the truth in love, we are to grow up in all aspects into Him, who is the head, even Christ, from whom the whole body, being fitted and held together by that which every joint supplies, according to the proper working of each individual part, causes the growth of the body for the building up of itself in love (Eph. 4:11-16).

Individually and corporately we are to be moving toward maturity in the Christian life. The apostle Paul was an excellent example of someone who did just that. Therefore, after listing some of the difficulties he endured for the Lord he could testify:

> Therefore, we do not lose heart, but though our outer man is decaying, yet our inner man is being renewed day by day. (II Cor. 4:16).

How are you doing? Is your inner man being renewed day by day? Have you passed through infancy and adolescence to spiritual maturity? Are you growing up in all aspects into Christ? Are you helping the whole

14

body to be built up so as to effectively carry on the work of Christ?

It is my contention that most of us are not growing spiritually as we should. Thus the church both local and universal is not growing spiritually as it should. The result is that the church is failing to make the impact on our society which God intended. John MacMillan addresses this situation in his book, *The Authority Of The Believer*.

> . . . the spread of an almost wholly secularized education is quietly doing away with scriptural standards . . . Our wealth and social culture have not made us thankful to the Giver of all good, but have centered us upon the material things of the world, and have produced a self-suffering that quite ignores our dependence upon the Creator of all . . . More serious still is the attitude of large sections of the church toward the state of the heathen. No longer are these concerned about the lost souls which wander in darkness; their thought is centered on raising their social status and meeting their intellectual and physical needs . . . Christ, in their view, has degenerated into a Superman, an example which in their own feeble strength they seek to follow.

MacMillan's next statement is significant: "To meet the situation, the Church of Christ needs a new conception of prayer."[1]

Indeed, it is my further contention that the reason we individually and corporately are not growing as we ought spiritually and thus not impacting on the world as we could is that we have failed to avail ourselves of the means for growth God has placed at our disposal, not least of which is prayer.

When I asked members of the Kingsway congregation to rate their spiritual satisfaction level on a scale of 0 to 10, 71% rated themselves five or less. However, in the same poll completed by 537 people, I learned that only 36% had a daily devotional time, over 50% prayed less than five minutes per day, and 54% read their Bible no more than once a week. It should be quite obvious that lack of attention to Christian disciplines is at least one of the reasons people are not growing spiritually.

You might be interested in knowing that I distributed the same survey to 100 Indianapolis area ministers. Oh, yes, they did better: 61% had daily devotions, and 82% studied the Scriptures for personal growth at least several times a week. Yet that means 39% didn't have a daily quiet time and 18% studied God's Word no more than once a week. Furthermore, 13.5% of the preachers spent less than five minutes a day in prayer.

One preacher commented, "One of the saddest things is that the people I am currently teaching are less active than myself in most all these areas. However, that in no way condones my lack of spirituality."

A well-known Christian college president shared how for years he had been working and ministering in the power of the flesh because he was so empty on the inside. He wasn't feeding the inner man. Only a return to a strong emphasis on prayer and a devotional life saved his ministry.

A famous gospel singer revealed that while he had been doing all the right things on the outside and having a seemingly successful ministry, his failure to feed the inner man and grow spiritually left him enslaved by pornography and with a wife slipping into alcoholism.

In my own life and ministry, there was a time I wished I had been taught more "practical things" about calling, organization, finance, and building programs. But after twenty-eight years of ministry, I wish I had been taught more about prayer, worship, meditation, and a personal walk with the Lord, for without those things – all the rest is just building on the sand.

In Meditations Of A Hermit Charles de Foucald writes,

> Later the soul will bring forth fruit exactly in the measure in which the inner life is developed in it. If there is no inner life, however great may be the zeal, the high attention, the hard work, no fruit will come forth . . . ONE CAN ONLY GIVE THAT WHICH ONE HAS.[2]

I believe we're ready. I believe there is a hunger for not just numerical growth (I'm all for that) but for the spiritual growth that gives it substance and meaning.

Someone wrote on their survey form, "I have never been asked these questions before. I am challenged. You have opened my eyes. I can now make changes." Another wrote, "When written down on paper, I realize how much my life lacks spiritually. I really have a desire to improve but need guidance."

Well, together let's seek that guidance as we look at some of the Christian disciplines God has provided for His children who are born to grow. In this introductory study, we need to look first at the Reversed Priorities or how the church has ignored the inward in favor of outward performance. Next we'll look at the Resultant

Problems. Most importantly, we'll look at the Required Principles to be applied if we are to grow.

THE REVERSED PRIORITIES

Jesus reserved His harshest judgment for the people who did all the right things outwardly. The Pharisees prayed, fasted, tithed, were concerned with cleanliness, gave great attention to carrying out their Jewish religious ceremonies in just the right way, and even evangelized. However, they divorced all those things from a right heart and a right motivation. It was all an outward performance. Thus Jesus thundered out:

> Woe to you, scribes and Pharisees, hypocrites, because you devour widows' houses even while for a pretense you make long prayers; therefore, you shall receive greater condemnation. Woe to you, scribes and Pharisees, hypocrites, because you travel about on sea and land to make one proselyte; and when he becomes one, you make him twice as much a child of hell as yourselves. (Matt. 23:14-15) . . . Woe to you, scribes and Pharisees, hypocrites! For you tithe mint and dill and cummin, and have neglected the weightier provisions of the law; justice and mercy and faithfulness; but these are the things you should have done without neglecting the others. (vs. 23) . . . Woe to you, scribes and Pharisees, hypocrites! For you clean the outside of the cup and of the dish, but inside they are full of robbery and self-indulgence. You blind Pharisee, first clean the inside of the cup and of the dish, so that the outside of it may become clean also. Woe to you, scribes and Pharisees, hypocrites! For you are like white-washed tombs which on the outside appear beautiful, but inside they are full of dead men's bones and of all uncleanness. Even so you too outwardly appear righteous to men, but

inwardly you are full of hypocrisy and lawlessness (vss. 25-28).

Oh, how we need to understand that God is first of all concerned with the heart of man, the spirit of man. Thousands of years ago He told Samuel, "God sees not as man sees, for man looks at the outward appearance, but the Lord looks at the heart" (I Sam. 16:7). After condemning the Pharisees for honoring God with their lips while their hearts were far from him, Jesus went on to say, "Not what enters into the mouth defiles the man, but what proceeds out of the mouth, that defiles the man" (Matt. 15:11).

Yet we still measure spirituality on the basis of outwardness. Outwardness goes to church, sings, prays, takes communion, reads so many chapters in the Bible, tithes, and tells others about Jesus. Now all these things are right and good and to be commended if they come from a right heart. But if the inner man is not right then all are pretense and hypocrisy. And the truth is, only you and God know for sure.

Calvin Miller has written an excellent book which I would urge you to read, _The Table Of Inwardness_. In it, he points out the dilemma that has caused us to emphasize the outward over the inward: "Discussing inwardness does not define it and exposing it is impossible."[3] He goes on to say, "Outwardness has for its greatest strength and greatest weakness the same thing: visibility. Likewise the strength and weakness of inwardness is the same: invisibility."[4]

God's priorities rest with the inward man. Yet we stress outward performance because it is the only thing we can see. Even our emphasis on Christian disciplines for spiritual growth can easily devolve into a modern day Phariseeism of "doing spiritual things." We must constantly be reminded that God's approval is what is important and that begins on the inside.

THE RESULTANT PROBLEMS

Our lack of concern for the inward man as reflected by our lack of attention to Christian disciplines has certainly had a negative impact on Christians everywhere. Gordon MacDonald addresses those consequences in Christians' lives in his book, *Restoring Your Spiritual Passion*. He used words like drained, dried out, distorted, devastated, disillusioned, defeated and disheartened to describe those consequences.[5] Does that sound like you? Have you been there? Notice that all of these are inward conditions.

I wrote to a number of Christian leaders across the country asking them to reflect on the state of the church as related to our lack of attention to spiritual disciplines. Ken Idleman, President of Ozark Christian College in Joplin, Missouri, cited five problems.

1. THE LACK OF GROWTH IN THE CHURCHES. He related this to a lack of boldness in our witness.
2. A LACK OF UNITY AMONG LOCAL CHURCH LEADERS. Ken tied this to a breakdown in the bonding influence of the spiritual disciplines.
3. A LACK OF SECURITY WITH RESPECT TO SALVATION. Only a daily renewal of our faith can produce a daily reality of security about our salvation.
4. A LACK OF COMMITMENT TO MISSION. Many Christians do not have a sense of mission. They don't feel a calling

from God with respect to their own personal ministry. The doctrine of the priesthood of all believers suffers when the rank and file of the priesthood is not understanding of what it means to have a living, personal relationship with Christ.
5. MORAL FAILURE AND BURNOUT IN LEADERSHIP. Ken suggests this is due to a breakdown in the spiritual disciplines. He writes, "I am persuaded that it is spiritual dryness or stagnancy which produces the moral and/or emotional cave-ins which are plaguing church leadership.[6]

Ken Idleman is correct on every count. However, he has identified just a few of the problems that have resulted from our lack of emphasis on the inner man. Bob Yawberg, minister of the Broadway Christian Church in Fort Wayne, Indiana, writes, "The church is in a horrible spiritual decline. It is not that spiritual resources aren't available but that we have forgotten where to find help; the church seems to be majoring in corporate business procedures and totally forgetting the power of the Holy Spirit."[7]

Brothers and sisters, he is right. There is an urgent need for revival and spiritual awakening in our land, our church, our lives. But it must begin with each of us individually as we seek personal, spiritual renewal through growth in the inner man.

REQUIRED PRINCIPLES

How is this to be accomplished? In the next chapters we'll be going into greater detail but for the moment, let me share some basic principles that are essential to our spiritual growth.

First, let it be made clear that Christian growth is the

work of the Holy Spirit. Apart from Him, all our human efforts would be vain strivings. Paul testifies to that in his own life in I Corinthians 2:12-16:

> Now we have received, not the spirit of the world, but the Spirit who is from God, that we might know the things freely given to us by God, which things we also speak, not in words taught by human wisdom, but in those taught by the Spirit, combining spiritual thoughts with spiritual words. But a natural man does not accept the things of the Spirit of God; for they are foolishness to him, and he cannot understand them, because they are spiritually appraised. But he who is spiritual appraises all things, yet he himself is appraised by no man. For who has known the mind of the Lord, that he should instruct Him? But we have the mind of Christ.

So the life of spiritual growth and vitality is the life that is lived by the power of and in dependency on the Spirit of God. Romans 8 is a great chapter that pictures a growing Christian experiencing victory. It speaks of walking "according to the Spirit" and setting our minds on "the things of the Spirit." Paul says, "The mind set on the Spirit is life and peace." He also speaks of being given life by the Spirit, being led by the Spirit, and the Spirit bearing "witness with our spirit that we are children of God." The growing Christian is walking in the Spirit.

Secondly, a growing Christian fills his life with positive goodness. It was Fosdick who wrote, " . . . a soul unoccupied by a positive devotion is sure to be occupied by spiritual demons."[8] Fosdick reminds us of the story of Ulysses. Perhaps you remember that when he passed the Isle of Sirens, he had his men tie him to the

22

mast and fill their ears with wax so that they might not hear the alluring sounds of the sirens. What a reflection of man's negative attempts at goodness. However, when Orpheus sailed past the Isle of Sirens, he was indifferent to their music. You see, he too was a musician and could make music so much more beautiful than the sirens that their music had no appeal. So it is that no amount of negative goodness can cause us to grow; but a life filled with positive goodness and disciplines will grow more and more into Christ-likeness.

Thirdly, we need to realize that busyness is the enemy of spirituality or spiritual growth. Comments on the Christian Disciplines Survey bore this out. "My greatest frustration of my inner spiritual life centers around time. There seems to be so many things pulling at my time." "God has been convicting me about being too busy even though I am doing good things." I need more power to control my schedule so that busyness does not prevent spiritual nurturing and discipleship." Preachers responding to the same survey agreed. "My biggest battle is preventing a horrendous schedule from interfering with my devotional life." "Consistency is the key! Not permitting the 'tyranny of the urgent' to push aside quality time in word, prayer, and fasting is a constant struggle." I can only agree and I think you can, too.

A fourth principle is simply that discipline is necessary for spiritual growth. There are no shortcuts. Elton Trueblood writes, "Without the discipline of time we spoil the next day the night before; and without the discipline of prayer, we are likely to end by having practically no experience of the divine-human encounter.

However compassionate we may be with ourselves, we dare not be soft or indulgent with ourselves. Excellence comes at a price, and one of the major prices is that of inner control."[9] When my son and daughter played in the Avon Marching Black and Gold, they practiced literally hundreds of hours in order to perfect their show. The one who would be a successful athlete must be willing to discipline his body by regular exercise and by abstaining from certain harmful things. Trueblood points out, "With one concerted voice, the giants of the devotional life apply the same principle to the whole of life with the dictum: Discipline is the price of freedom."

Let me add one final principle in the form of a warning. We must not allow the use of Christian disciplines for spiritual growth to devolve into a legalistic system. The Pharisees took good things and used them for evil because the purpose was lost and the externals were emphasized. Spiritual pride set in. Furthermore, they bound those externals on others as a sign of spirituality when it was nothing more nor less than legalistic conformity. Richard Foster has written what is to me the finest book on Christian disciplines of this century, *Celebration Of Discipline*. In it he emphasizes this very warning. He writes:

> When the disciplines degenerate into law, they are used to manipulate and control people . . . If we are to progress in the spiritual walk so that the disciplines are a blessing and not a curse, we must come to the place in our lives where we lay down the everlasting burden of needing to manage others . . . Without laws the disciplines are primarily an internal work and it is impossible to control an inner work.[10]

Remember the words of Paul, " . . . the letter (of the law) kills, but the Spirit gives life" (II Cor. 3:6).

CONCLUSION

Christian, you were born again to grow! The Lord wants you to grow. But too many of us have not been availing ourselves of the resources He has provided for our spiritual growth. Maybe you've been focusing all your attention on outward performance. I hope you'll see the need of reversing your priorities. For if the inner man grows, the outward performance must follow. I hope you've come to see the problems that result from lack of spiritual growth and that you simply cannot be satisfied without doing something about it. I also hope you've understood the principles we've introduced that are requirements if we are to grow: the necessity of walking in the Spirit; the need for positive goodness; the difficulty busyness presents; the absolute necessity of disciplines; and the warning against allowing Christian disciplines to devolve into a legalistic system.

Over the last few years, I've come to know and appreciate L.D. Campbell, pastor-teacher at the First Church of Christ in Florence, Kentucky. He shares this testimony:

> I feel deeply about the quiet time, because it has saved my ministry and has saved me. I must also say, I had to learn it the hard way myself. I was not taught in college how to feed myself, or if they tried to teach me, I didn't listen. I was taught how to preach and pastor, not how to minister to myself through the Word and prayer.

25

I was almost ready to give up the ministry, because I was spiritually drained. For years it had been MY ministry, MY personality. I had given out and was completely empty. I had decided to become an undertaker.

I went to Asheville, North Carolina, to a Ben Lippen Conference to hear Dr. Stephen Olford. I either had to repent or resign. I decided to repent. After the conference, I was vacationing at my home, so I borrowed the key to my little home church and on my face in a little room off the vestibule, I repented and gave myself and my ministry to the Lordship of Jesus Christ and dedicated myself to a devotional life. That was in 1971 or 1972. It has made all the difference in the world. There have been times when I wanted to be an undertaker, but I've learned to charge my spiritual batteries in a time of personal prayer and worship.[11]

One of my favorite gospel singers is Larnelle Harris. A song he wrote, recorded, and released in 1986 challenged, convicted, and encouraged me. He shares it as a personal testimony:

There He was just waiting
In our old familiar place
An empty spot beside Him
Where once I used to wait
To be filled with strength and wisdom
For the battle of the day.
I would have passed Him by again
But I clearly heard Him say,

"I miss my time with you,
Those moments together.
I need to be with you each day
And it hurts me when you say
You're too busy, busy tryin' to serve me,
But how can you serve me
When your spirit's empty . . .

There's a longing in my heart
Wanting more than just a part.
It's true . . . I miss my time with you."

Then Larnelle sings:

What will I have to offer?
How can I truly care?
My efforts have no meaning
When Your presence isn't there.
But You'll provide the power
If I take time to pray.
So I'll stay right beside You
And you'll never have to say
"I miss my time with you."[12]

God is there. He wants to spend time with you. His
Holy Spirit wants to help you grow. Will you let Him?

THOUGHT QUESTIONS:

1. How much have you grown in the Lord since you
first became a Christian?

2. How much have you grown spiritually this past
year?

3. How do you feel about spending time with the
Lord?

4. When was the last time you really felt close to the
Lord? Why was that?

5. What do you believe is holding you back from
growing more spiritually?

6. Is failure to practice the Christian disciplines a
major factor?

7. What made the greatest impact on you personally in this chapter "Born To Grow?"

8. What specific things do you plan to do as a result of this study?

ASSIGNMENTS:

Make a list of ten events in your spiritual life in the order in which they occurred and note your age at each event. Think of persons, organizations, books, spiritual experiences, etc. which are at the center of possible events.

Write out your personal testimony. Every Christian has one. (What it was like before Christ, how I came to Christ, and what it's like since I gave my life to Him).

SCRIPTURE REFERENCES:

I Peter 1:23
I Peter 2:1-3
II Peter 3:18
Eph. 4:11-16
II Cor. 4:16
Matt. 23:14-15,23,25-28
I Sam. 16:7
Matt. 15:11
I Cor. 2:12-16
Rom. 8:1-17
I Cor. 3:6

RECOMMENDED READING:

Celebration of Discipline by Richard Foster
Restoring Your Spiritual Passion by Gordon MacDonald
The Table of Inwardness by Calvin Miller
The Pursuit of God by A.W. Tozer

SOMETHING TO THINK ON:

"Outwardness has for its greatest strength and greatest weakness the same thing: visibility. Likewise the strength and weakness of inwardness is the same: invisibility."

–Calvin Miller

Chapter Two

GROWING THROUGH PRAYER

God wills for His people to pray. In the first verse of
the eighteenth chapter of his gospel, Luke tells us that
Jesus told a parable to show that we should pray at all
times and not lose heart. In I Thessalonians 5:17, Paul
exhorts us to "pray without ceasing." In I Timothy 2:1,
he says, "First of all, then, I urge that entreaties and
prayers, petitions and thanksgivings, be made on behalf
of all men." In verse 8 he adds, "Therefore, I want the
men in every place to pray . . . "

Yes, God wills for His people to pray; but not only do
we often fall short in the practice of prayer, but in the
intention of prayer as well. Songwriter Larry Bryant
underscored the latter in his parody on prayer, "Shop-

ping List."

> Lord, I need to talk to you – there's so much on my
> mind;
> So many burdens make it hard to know just where to
> start.
> Thank you for your family, your mercy, and your love.
> Now on to more important things,
> I'll give my magic lamp a rub.
> Give me this, I want that, bless me Lord I pray.
> Grant me what I think I need to make it through the day.
> Make me wealthy, keep me healthy, fill in what I miss
> On my never ending shopping list.
> Lord you've been so good to me, how could I ask for
> more?
> But since you said to ask, I will, cause what else is
> prayer for?
> The cattle on a thousand hills, they all belong to you;
> I don't need any cows right now but something else
> might do.
> I made my list and I checked it twice,
> If I got it all it would sure be nice.
> I want a nice white smile on a perfect face,
> And perfect hair that will stay in place.
> I want a smaller nose and a single chin,
> And a figure like a perfect ten,
> And a mom that never yells or screams,
> And hips that fit in designer jeans,
> And a tennis court and a heated pool,
> I could use it, Lord, as a witnessing tool,
> And a color TV and a VCR,
> And Jesus plates on a brand new car.
> Give me this, I want that, bless me Lord I pray.
> Grant me what I think I need to make it through the day.
> Make me wealthy, keep me healthy, fill in what I miss
> On my never ending shopping list.[13]

Yes, prayer is asking and receiving, but it is so much
more. If we see prayer only or primarily as some sort of

cosmic shopping list or wish list, then we have missed the point. Prayer is communion and communication between the Spirit of God and the spirit of man. It is the primary means man has of drawing close to God and growing in the spiritual life.

Jack Taylor shares these four perspectives on our prayer life:

1. No believer's spiritual life will rise to stay above the level of his praying.

2. No church's ultimate effectiveness will rise to stay above the level of its corporate prayer life.

3. No church's corporate prayer life will be greater than the personal prayer lives of those who make up its constituency.

4. No believer's prayer life will rise to stay above the level of his or her own personal, regular, daily time of worship with God.[14]

If Taylor is right, and I believe he is on all four counts, then this topic has tremendous significance for all of us, significance even greater than we can begin to comprehend.

It is not my intention to even touch on all the areas of prayer that merit our consideration. It is my intention, however, to look at prayer as a means of spiritual growth and hopefully to consider some motivational factors which will encourage us in the practice of the discipline of prayer.

THE PURPOSE OF PRAYER

We usually think of prayer as asking things of God or

at least talking to Him, thanking Him and praising Him. However, let me suggest that prayer is first of all LISTENING to God. In prayer God has our attention. We don't have to ask for His attention, we already have it. Ours is not the problem of getting God to listen but of our being too busy, unconcerned, or preoccupied to listen to Him. Take time to listen to God and you will find Him eager to share with you on the most personal or intimate of levels. Take time to listen to God and you will find yourself far more ready and willing to accept His answers to your prayers even though they may be contrary to your desires or expectations. God sometimes answers our prayers with an immediate, "Yes," sometimes with an immediate, "No," sometimes with, "Wait, be patient," and sometimes with, "I've got something far better in mind." Only as we learn to listen can we properly discern and accept His answer.

All of this leads to a second purpose in prayer, that of entering into close, intimate fellowship with God. A couple from California were driving across Texas when they spotted a tornado. Terrified, they got out of their car and lay flat in a ditch. The twister was headed right for them but at the last moment veered away and across a field where it demolished a small wooden house. The man and his wife ran on trembling legs to the house which now consisted of a pile of kindling wood and a hole in the ground. Peering into the hole they saw an old man, his eyes tightly closed, holding on for dear life to a timber that had once supported the floor of his house. "Hey down there, are you all right?" the woman called to him. The old man opened his eyes, looked around and said, "I guess so." "Was there anyone else with you?" the woman asked. The old-timer replied, "Just me and God, and we were having an urgent conversation." ✗

We don't have to wait for a tornado to strike in order to learn that God wants us to enter into a close, intimate, personal relationship with Him. The deepest level of your spirit is the level at which God's Holy Spirit communes with you, Christian. When you pray, your spirit and the Holy Spirit enter into a spiritual communion.

In a book of letters that children have addressed to God, a little boy named Eric writes, "Dear God, is it okay to talk to you even when I don't want anything? Love, Eric." It's not just okay, Eric, it's what God wants. He wants all of us to enter into a loving, trusting relationship with Him developed and expressed by prayer.

I love my children and I'll do my best to see that their needs are met. Most often I am aware of those needs even before they talk to me about them. Yet, it is the communication, the fellowship, and the communion which I enjoy with my children that makes me all the more desirous of meeting their needs. Praying, "Our Father," is not only a special privilege but denotes a very special relationship.

Furthermore, prayer is for the purpose of being in the will of God. In John 15:7 Jesus said, "If you abide in Me, and My words abide in you, ask whatever you wish, and it shall be done for you." Prayer and abiding in Christ, and doing the will of God go hand in hand. If we live in Him, and if His words are a part of our lives, then we can confidently petition God. But only "If!" Only then will we know what to ask of God. Thus the discipline of prayer is a primary means of spiritual growth, for it leads us to seek and to do the will of the Lord.

Actually, sincere Christian prayer cannot be offered outside the context of a prayerful life. We live as we pray and we pray as we live. If we live in the spirit of self-service where all that is important is what we want, then we will pray in the expectation that we can manipulate God. But if we pray abiding in Christ, we will pray according to God's will. Jesus taught us to pray, "Thy kingdom come. Thy will be done, on earth as it is in heaven." Sincerely prayed, that is an affirmation that we are bringing our lives into harmony with God's will. "Not my will but thine be done."

The story is so old, I'm almost embarrassed to retell it but it makes the point.

A young man is making a difficult mountain climb. Suddenly he loses his footing and begins to slip. Frantically he grasps a fragile bush growing from a crevice as he is left dangling in mid-air hundreds of feet above the ground. He begins to call out, "Help! Help! Is anyone up there?" After what seems like an eternity Jesus appears just above him. "Do you need help?" "Master," cries the young man, "Please help me!" "Do you really want my help?" Jesus asks. "Yes, Master, without your help, I am doomed. Please, I will do whatever you ask." "Well then," Jesus replies, "First, you must let go." There is a long pause after which the young man cries out, "Help, isn't there someone else up there?" Prayer aligns our will with the will of God.

God's purpose in prayer involves far more than we've mentioned. We've not even dealt with the most obvious, prayer as a basis for blessing or a means of having our needs met. However, I want to mention only one other aspect of the purpose of prayer, and this one is especially important as it relates to purpose: prayer is an expression of faith and a means of strengthening that faith.

Faith is a precondition of prayer. James 1:6-7 says, "Let him ask in faith without any doubting, for the one who doubts is like the surf of the sea driven and tossed by the wind. For let not that man expect that he will receive anything from the Lord." Even the father of the demonized boy of Mark 9 cried out, "I do believe; help my unbelief." What do you suppose happened when Jesus responded to his plea and helped his son and delivered his son of the unclean spirit? Don't you think that man was strengthened in his faith? Faith exercised becomes a stronger faith. That was the case with Abraham who, "By faith . . . when he was called, obeyed . . . and he went out not knowing where he was going" (Heb. 11:8). Later he had faith when God told him that even at one hundred years of age he would have a son. Romans 4:20 tells us, "He did not waver in unbelief but grew strong in faith . . . " Likewise, prayer as an exercise of faith becomes a means whereby that faith is strengthened. I have seen God respond again and again in response to a prayer of faith from His children and I cannot help but believe!

THE PRACTICE OF PRAYER

We can understand everything there is to be understood about the purpose of prayer, but it is only as we
practice prayer that those purposes are fulfilled. And
when it comes to the practice of prayer, no one set a
better example for us than the Lord Jesus Christ Himself. In Mark the first chapter, we read of a day in which
Jesus called His first apostles, healed many sick people,
cast out demons, caused such a sensation that crowds of
people pressed in on Him, taught people about the
Kingdom of God and ministered late into the evening. It
must have been an exhausting day. Yet Mark observes
in verse thirty-five, "And in the early morning, while it
was still dark, He arose and went out and departed to a
lonely place, and was praying there."

Repeatedly we find such references in the gospel
accounts. Again and again Jesus withdrew to pray.
Before He chose His disciples, Jesus needed to be alone
at prayer. On the Mount of Transfiguration, where He
had to make a very important decision about His ministry, Jesus needed to be alone at prayer. In the upper
room with His disciples, Jesus spent much time in
prayer. In the Garden of Gethsemane and on the cross,
from the first day of His ministry to the last, Jesus
needed to be at prayer.

Please note that while prayer was important at those
momentous milestones of Christ's life, it also permeated

every facet of His everyday life. We read of Jesus praying when He healed people, when He ate a meal, when He took a trip, before He taught, when in the temple and on and on. It appears that it was His regular practice to spend the early morning hours in prayer to His Heavenly Father.

But what of us? What of modern day man's practice of prayer? According to the response to the Spiritual Disciplines Survey, only 4.4% of our Kingsway people prayed thirty or more minutes per day. Only 16.5% of the area preachers did. Meanwhile, 54% of our people prayed less than five minutes per day as did 13.5% of the preachers. The survey revealed that 70% of our people didn't even keep a prayer list. Brethren, something is frightfully wrong.

There are more books on prayer than on any other Christian discipline. Sermons are preached, seminars held, programs organized, but the people of God do not pray. Dr. W. F. Lown wrote:

> Somewhere there must come a cessation of reading and preaching about prayer, and let there be an initiating of a vibrant prayer lifestyle. People, I suspect, are more likely to eagerly go to seminars on prayer than they are to engage in the laborious and tiring task of praying itself. Prayer is hard work. It is also dangerous. We need to be sure that we want God to answer the prayers we are offering to Him. Do we really want to pray for God to make us more like Jesus in a world which spat upon Him, scorned Him and finally crucified Him? Do we?[15]

Dr. Lown shared an experience which again underscores the pathetic state of the church in regard to the practice of prayer. He was to lead the devotional periods of the planning meeting for the North American Christian Convention. He was assigned the theme of prayer. He decided it would be more profitable to spend time praying rather than talking about it. So they spent the thirty minutes allotted for each day in prayer. One day, however, he asked each man (over 100 Christian leaders) to jot down on a piece of paper the approximate number of minutes they spent each day in prayer. The shocking average which he reported back the next day was THREE MINUTES per day.

Lest you think that was a fluke, the workbook, *Christian Disciplines*, from InterVarsity Press reports: "A lack of time or quality in prayer seems to be an almost universal frustration among Christians. A recent survey of American pastors reveals that the average pastor spends only three minutes a day in personal prayer."[16]

Let us take no comfort in the fact that others may be even worse off than ourselves. Spiritual growth and power will not be experienced with such prayerlessness. The great giant of prayer, E.M. Bounds, wrote:

> Non-praying is lawless, discord, anarchy. The whole force of Bible statement is to increase our faith in the doctrine that prayer affects God, secures favor from God, which can be secured in no other way, and which will not be bestowed if we do not pray.[17]

THE POWER OF PRAYER

Part of the tragedy of prayerlessness is the power we

deny ourselves and the church. God makes this tremendous offer in Jeremiah 33:3, "Call to Me, and I will answer you, and I will tell you great and mighty things which you do not know." The Bible is filled with examples of people who called upon God and who experienced great and mighty things. Abraham prayed for a child in his old age and Isaac was born. Abraham interceded on behalf of Sodom and God agreed to spare the city if ten righteous persons could be found there. Rachel prayed that she could have children and Joseph was born. Joshua prayed for more daylight and the sun stood still in relation to the earth. Gideon prayed for confirmation of God's will through the fleece and God complied. Elijah prayed for fire from heaven and it came and consumed the sacrifice, the wood, the stones, the dust, and the water on Mt. Carmel. Elisha prayed for the son of the Shunamite woman and the boy was resurrected. Hezekiah prayed for healing from a terminal illness and was granted fifteen more years of life. Daniel prayed and was delivered from the lions' den. Jonah prayed and was delivered from the belly of the great fish. Peter prayed and was able to walk on the water. The church prayed and Peter was released from prison. Paul prayed and he and all the other passengers were saved from the shipwreck in the midst of a terrible storm. THERE IS POWER IN PRAYER!!! The Bible is filled with examples.

However, church history and modern-day experiences are also filled with such examples. Do yourself a favor and read *The Life And Diary Of David Brainerd* as edited by Jonathan Edwards. His whole life was a life of prayer and that enabled him to accomplish more for God in twenty-nine years than most of us would in ninety. E.M. Bounds writes of Brainerd, "He was with God mightily in prayer, and God was with him mightily."[18] The complete transformation of the Indians among whom he worked from debased heathenism to devout Christian in belief and practice is a testimony to the power of prayer as practiced by this godly man.

Reading the autobiography of George Mueller will also thrill your soul. He cared for thousands of orphans over a period of seventy years without ever asking anyone for assistance but God and every need was supplied, often in the most unexpected of ways. On one occasion Mueller traveled to Canada to speak. Dense fog slowed the oceanliner till it sat motionless. Mueller went to the captain and said, "I must be in Toronto by Sunday." The captain replied that there was no way they could move in the thick fog without endangering everyone on board. Mueller replied, "I understand, but in forty years of Christian service, I have not failed to keep an appointment!" He then asked the captain to join him in prayer. They knelt together and Mueller calmly asked God to lift the fog. The captain started to pray also but Mueller stopped him saying, "You need not pray. You do not believe." However, when they walked out to the deck, the captain believed. The fog had completely lifted.[19]

Let one more story suffice in illustrating my point. Rees Howells was a dedicated twentieth-century intercessor who did a great work for the Lord during the trying years of World War II. He tells of the miracle of

Salerno. Allied troops had landed in Salerno, Italy, in 1943 in preparation for the march on Rome. Here is an eyewitness account of Howells' activities that night:

> We had the first evening prayer meeting as usual in the conference hall, and gathered again at 9:45 P.M. The meeting had a solemn tone from the outset. The Director, Mr. Howells, voice trembling with the burden of his message and scarcely audible, said, "The Lord has burdened me between the meetings with the invasion at Salerno. I believe our men are in great danger of losing their hold."

Howells then called the congregation of Bible students to prayer. It was not an ordinary prayer time. Prayer was intense and urgent, and in the greatest sense, true prevailing prayer. Howells relates, "The Spirit took hold of us and suddenly broke right through in the prayers, and we found ourselves praising and rejoicing, believing that God had heard and answered. We could not go on praying any longer, so we rose ... the Spirit witnessing in all our hearts that God had wrought some miraculous intervention in Italy. The victory was so outstanding that I looked at the clock as we rose to sing. It was the stroke of 11:00 P.M."

The story continues with amazing tribute to the value of persistent prayer. Several days later one of the local newspapers displayed the headline in large print, "The Miracle of Salerno." A front line reporter gave his personal account of the battle. He was with the advanced troops in the Salerno invasion on Monday. The enemy was advancing rapidly, and increasing devastation was evident. It was obvious that unless a miracle happened the city would be lost. British troops had insufficient strength to stop the advance until the beachhead was established. Suddenly, with no reason, firing ceased and deathlike stillness settled. The reporter describes the next few moments, "We waited in breathless anticipation but nothing happened. I looked at my watch – It was ELEVEN O'CLOCK AT NIGHT. Still we waited, but still nothing happened; and nothing happened all night, but those hours made all the difference to the invasion. By morning the beachhead was established."[20]

THE PROCEDURE OF PRAYER

How can we pray like that? What is our pattern for prayer? Immediately our Lord's Model Prayer comes to mind.

Pray, then, in this way:
"Our Father who art in heaven,
Hallowed by Thy name.
Thy kingdom come.
Thy will be done,
On earth as it is in heaven.
Give us this day our daily bread.
And forgive us our debts, as we also have
    forgiven our debtors.
And do not lead us into temptation, but deliver us
    from evil. For Thine is the kingdom, and the
    power, and the glory, forever, Amen."

We can also learn a great deal about prayer and expand our own prayer life by reading and praying the prayers others have written. That has been one of the most enriching aspects of my own prayer life in recent years.

It is important to remember that prayer has many aspects. Matthew Henry is credited with the acrostic

"ACTS" – adoration, confession, thanksgiving, and supplication. When it comes to supplication or petition, there is surely no shortage of objects of prayer. Your prayer list can include family, church, church leaders, family needs, church needs, the backslidden, the lost, the sick, missionaries, governmental leaders and our enemies. Pray for personal needs such as overcoming temptation, developing character, relationships, work, study, self-discipline, spiritual growth or whatever else the need might be.

The time, the place, the posture, the duration, and the vocabulary of prayer no one else can prescribe for you. Any time and any place is appropriate for prayer although it will be helpful in developing a prayer life if you set aside a certain time and place.

The posture of prayer is entirely a matter of individual preference as illustrated by "The Prayer of Cyrus Brown."

"The proper way for a man to pray,"
Said Deacon Lemuel Keyes,
"And the only proper attitude
Is down upon his knees."
"No, I should say the way to pray,"
Said Reverend Dr. Wise,
"Is standing straight with outstretched arms,
And rapt and upturned eyes.
"Oh, no, no, no," said Elder Slow,
"Such posture is too proud:
A man should pray with eyes fast-closed
And head contritely bowed."
"It seems to me his hands should be
Serenely clasped in front,
With both thumbs pointing to the ground,"
Said Reverend Dr. Blunt.

"Last year I fell in Hidgekin's well
Headfirst," said Cyrus Brown,
"With both my feet a-stickin' up
And head a-pointin' down:
"And I made a prayer right then and there,
The best prayer I ever said,
The prayingest prayer I ever prayed
A-standin' on my head."[21]

The duration can vary from a short "arrow prayer" when you think of someone, when you address a letter, or when you read about someone, to a period of hours on your knees when the burden of a great crisis or major decision is upon your heart. But let me suggest as an arbitrary figure that according to our survey would challenge most of us – let me urge you to commit yourself to fifteen minutes a day in prayer.

When it comes to vocabulary, God already knows what you're thinking anyway; you don't have to try to impress Him. Just be yourself. Besides, there will be times when words aren't even necessary. Paul tells us in Romans 8:26, "In the same way the Spirit also helps our weaknesses; for we do not know how to pray as we should, but the Spirit Himself intercedes for us with groanings too deep for words."

CONCLUSION

I have not always prayed as I ought. I certainly have not arrived now. But I am moving in the right direction and I am learning that prayer encourages prayer; that the more you pray the more you want to pray. Consequently, I am finding a closer walk with the Lord than ever before, a peace that is more complete, and a discipline of life that is helping me to make progress in many areas where previously I've been frustrated.

Think of it, as God's children, all of the grace, strength, and character of God the Father and of Christ, His Son are ours. Begin now to appropriate by faith through prayer what has been yours all along. And remember that this access is provided only to you as God 's child through the blood of Christ shed for you on Calvary. "We have confidence to enter the holy place by the blood of Jesus" (Heb. 10:19). Therefore, our Lord is glorified and honored by the prayers of His people.

THOUGHT QUESTIONS:

1. What have been your primary difficulties in praying?

2. What do you believe to be the primary purpose of prayer?

3. How does communion with God differ from the experience of human friendship?

4. If God is all-knowing and all-good, then why do we need to pray?

5. Why doesn't God always answer our prayers in the affirmative?

6. Do you feel free to tell God everything? What would you rather keep to yourself?

7. How do our attitudes about our parents affect the way we relate to God in prayer?

8. How do prayer and "abiding in Christ" relate to each other?

9. On what are most of your prayers centered?

10. How do you respond to Jack Taylor's statement that "no believer's spiritual life will rise to stay above the level of his praying?"

11. What specific, practical suggestions regarding methods for prayer have helped you most?

12. In what specific ways do you see prayer being linked to spiritual growth?

ASSIGNMENTS:

Using the acrostic ACTS (adoration, confession, thanksgiving, and supplication) as a guide, write out a short prayer including all four elements.

Make an evangelistic prayer list of ten people you want to see won to Christ or added to the local church and begin to pray for them every day.

PRAYER EXAMPLES:

"Lord, I do not know what to ask of you; only you know what I need. I simply present myself to you; I open my heart to you. I have no other desire than to accomplish your will. Teach me to pray. Amen."
                    –Francois Fenelon in LITTLE BOOK OF PRAYERS

"Blessed heavenly Father, in the name of the Lord Jesus Christ I desire to walk in the Spirit today. I recognize that only as He lives the life of the Lord Jesus Christ in me will I be able to escape the works of my flesh. I desire the Holy

Spirit to bring all of the work of the crucifixion and the resurrection of Christ into my life today. I pray that the Holy Spirit may produce His fruit within my whole being and shed abroad in my heart great love for the heavenly Father, for the Lord Jesus Christ, and for others about me. Forgive me, dear Holy Spirit, for all times I have grieved or quenched You. Enable me to respond to Your grace and to be sensitive to Your voice. Grant to me the desire and enablement to be obedient to Your precious Word. Grant me discernment to avoid being deceived by false spirits. I desire that the Holy Spirit fill all of my being with His presence and control me by faith. I trust my victory over the flesh today completely into the hands of the Holy Spirit as I let Him take control of me. In the name of the Lord Jesus Christ, I receive all the fullness of the Holy Spirit into all areas of my being today. Amen."

–Mark Bubeck from THE ADVERSARY

"Ah, Lord God, Thou holy Lover of my soul, when Thou comest into my soul, all that is within me shall rejoice. Thou art my Glory and the exultation of my heart; Thou art my Hope and Refuge in the day of my trouble. Set me free from all evil passions, and heal my heart of all inordinate affections; that, being inwardly cured and thoroughly cleansed, I may be made fit to love, courageous to suffer, steady to persevere. Nothing is sweeter than Love, nothing more courageous, nothing fuller nor better in heaven and earth; because Love is born of God, and cannot rest but in God, above all created things. Let me love Thee more than myself, nor love myself but for Thee. Amen."

–Thomas a Kempis (1379-1471)
from THE MEANING OF PRAYER

THOU GOD OF ALL GRACE,
Thou hast given me a saviour,
produce in me a faith to live by him,
                    to make him all my desire,
                        all my hope,
                        all my glory.

May I enter him as my refuge,

49

build on him as my foundation,
walk in him as my way,
follow him as my guide,
conform to him as my example,
receive his instructions as my prophet,
rely on his intercession as my high priest,
obey him as my king.
May I never be ashamed of him or his words,
    but joyfully bear his reproach,
    never displease him by unholy or imprudent
      conduct,
    never count it a glory if I take it patiently
    when buffeted for a fault,
    never make the multitude my model,
    never delay when thy Word invites me to advance.
May thy dear Son preserve me from this present evil
    world,
    so that its smiles never allure,
    nor its frowns terrify,
    nor its vices defile,
    nor its errors delude me.
May I feel that I am a stranger and a pilgrim on earth,
    declaring plainly that I seek a country,
    my title to it becoming daily more clear,
    my meekness for it more perfect,
    my foretastes of it more abundant;
    and whatsoever I do may it be done in the Saviour's
    name.
    –A Puritan Prayer from THE VALLEY OF VISION

"Use me then, my Saviour, for whatever purpose, and in whatever way, Thou mayest require. Here is my poor heart, an empty vessel; fill it with Thy grace. Here is my sinful and troubled soul; quicken it and refresh it with Thy love. Take my heart for Thine abode; my mouth to spread abroad the glory of Thy name; my love and all my powers, for the advancement of Thy believing people; and never suffer the steadfastness and confidence of my faith to abate—that so at all times I may be enabled from the heart to say, 'Jesus needs me, and I Him.' "

–D.L. Moody from THE MEANING OF PRAYER

"O God, I have tasted Thy goodness, and it has both satisfied me and made me thirsty for more. I am painfully conscious of my need of further grace. I am ashamed of my lack of desire. O God, the Triune God, I want to want Thee; I long to be filled with longing; I thirst to be made more thirsty still. Show me Thy glory, I pray Thee, that so I may know Thee indeed. Begin in mercy a new work of love within me. Say to my soul, 'Rise up, my love, my fair one, and come away.' Then give me grace to rise and follow Thee up from this misty lowland where I have wandered so long. In Jesus' name. Amen."

–A.W. Tozer from THE PURSUIT OF GOD

SCRIPTURE REFERENCES:

Luke 18:1ff	James 1:6-7	Matt. 6:9-13
I Tim. 2:1	Heb. 11:8	Rom. 8:26
John 15:7	Rom. 4:20	Heb. 10:19

RECOMMENDED READING:

The Kneeling Christian by an unknown Christian
No Easy Road by Dick Eastman
The Practice Of The Presence Of God by Brother
   Lawrence
With Christ In The School Of Prayer by Andrew Murray
Power Through Prayer by E.M. Bounds

QUOTABLE QUOTES:

"What the church needs today is not more machinery or better, not new organizations or more novel methods, but men whom the Holy Ghost can use – men of prayer, men mighty in prayer."

–E.M. Bounds

"The angel fetched Peter out of prison, but it was prayer fetched the angel."

–Thomas Watson

"You can do more than pray, after you have prayed, but you cannot do more than pray until you have prayed."

–John Bunyan

"More things are wrought by prayer than this world dreams of."

–Alfred Lord Tennyson

"We believe in prayer. Then why don't we pray? The real reason is, we have nothing to pray for. We have everything we want without praying. The supreme tragedy of most people is that they want so little and they are satisfied with almost nothing."

–Charles Allen

"And in the early morning, while it was still dark, He arose and went out and departed to a lonely place, and was praying there."

–Mark 1:35

Chapter Three

GROWING THROUGH CONFESSION

In II Samuel 11-12 we have recorded the story of a man whose life is an object lesson about guilt, confession, and forgiveness. One evening, David, King of Israel, walked out onto the roof of his palace (roofs were flat and used like a porch today). Looking down, he saw a beautiful young woman taking a bath. Seeing her, he wanted her. He sent for her and slept with her even though Bathsheba was the wife of one of David's soldiers.

She got pregnant and David tried to make it appear the child was fathered by her husband, Uriah, by ordering Uriah home from battle. However, Uriah was too good a soldier to disobey the military code forbidding sexual relations during a time of war. In desperation, David had Uriah assigned to the front lines where he was killed. After an appropriate period of mourning, David married Bathsheba.

Here was the King of Israel who had broken at least four of the Ten Commandments. God had declared through Moses, "You shall not murder . . . You shall not commit adultery . . . You shall not bear false witness against your neighbor . . . You shall not covet your neighbor's wife" (Exod. 20:13-14, 16-17). David had deliberately violated the deepest moral, ethical, and religious values of his nation and of his God.

David tried to forget about his sin. He tried to gloss it over like nothing had happened. However, deep down inside, his guilt ate away at his soul. When God finally sent the prophet Nathan to confront David with his sins, he was ready to repent of them and confess them. Thus we read in II Samuel 12:13, "David said to Nathan, 'I have sinned against the Lord.' And Nathan said to David, 'The Lord also has taken away your sin . . . ' "

Then David wrote the beautiful Psalm 51:

Be gracious to me, O God, according to Thy loving–
    kindness;
According to the greatness of Thy compassion blot out my
    transgressions.
Wash me thoroughly from my iniquity,
And cleanse me from my sin.
For I know my transgressions,
And my sin is ever before me.
Against Thee, Thee only, I have sinned,
And done what is evil in Thy sight,
So that Thou art justified when Thou doest speak,

And blameless when Thou dost judge.
  Behold, I was brought forth in iniquity,
And in sin my mother conceived me.
Behold, Thou dost desire truth in the innermost being,
And in the hidden part Thou wilt make me know wisdom.
  Purify me with hyssop, and I shall be clean;
Wash me, and I shall be whiter than snow.
Make me to hear joy and gladness,
Let the bones which Thou hast broken rejoice.
Hide Thy face from my sins,
And blot out all my iniquities.
Create in me a clean heart, O God,
And renew a steadfast spirit within me.
Do not cast me away from Thy presence,
And do not take Thy Holy Spirit from me.
Restore to me the joy of Thy salvation,
And sustain me with a willing spirit.
Then I will teach transgressors Thy ways,
And sinners will be converted to Thee.
  Deliver me from bloodguiltiness, O God, Thou God of my
    salvation;
Then my tongue will joyfully sing of Thy righteousness.
O Lord, open my lips,
That my mouth may declare Thy praise.
For Thou dost not delight in sacrifice, otherwise I would
    give it;
Thou art not pleased with burnt offering.
The sacrifices of God are a broken spirit;
A broken and a contrite heart, O God, Thou wilt not
    despise.

(Psa. 51:1-17)

What were the results of such confession and peni-
tence? Listen to the words of Psalm 32:

How blessed is he whose transgression is forgiven,
Whose sin is covered!
How blessed is the man to whom the Lord does not
    impute iniquity,

And in whose spirit there is no deceit!
  When I kept silent about my sin, my body wasted away
Through my groaning all day long.
For day and night Thy hand was heavy upon me;
My vitality was drained away as with the fever-heat of
    summer.
I acknowledged my sin to Thee,
And my iniquity I did not hide;
I said, 'I will confess my transgressions to the Lord;'
And Thou didst forgive the guilt of my sin.

(Psa. 32:1-5)

David's son, Solomon, was to state the principle concisely in Proverbs 28:13, "He who conceals his transgressions will not prosper, but he who confesses and forsakes them will find compassion." How tragic that so many of us haven't learned that and thus go on living with unconfessed sin and its accompanying guilt.

Unconfessed sin destroys a close, intimate relationship with God. As a boy growing up, when I had done something I knew to be wrong, I didn't want to be around my father. I felt guilty. I anticipated his punishment. But once the guilt was admitted and the wrong dealt with, a sense of relief and freedom filled my mind. So it is with our heavenly Father. If we knowingly hold on to that which displeases Him, a tremendous barrier is erected. Unconfessed sin destroys our desire to know God's will and to pray accordingly. Isaiah made that clear to the people of his day:

Behold, the Lord's hand is not so short
That it cannot save;
Neither is His ear so dull
That it cannot hear.

> But your iniquities have made a separation between you
> and your God,
> And your sins have hid His face from you, so that He does
> not hear.
>
> (Isa. 59:1-2)

However, unconfessed sin doesn't just hurt us spiritually. Warren Myers writes in his book on prayer, "Sin unacknowledged and unconfessed hinders not only our spiritual progress, but also our emotional well-being, and through that, our physical health." He goes on to mention heart disorders, high blood pressure, and acute indigestion as results of holding on to certain kinds of sins. He says, "Leading health authorities agree that the deeper causes of many illnesses are our emotional reactions to life."[22] David certainly found that to be true. "When I kept silent about my sin, my body wasted away . . . My vitality was drained away as with the fever-heat of summer" (Psa. 32:3-4).

Guilt can even kill. After his betrayal of Jesus, Judas' guilt was so great that he went out and hanged himself. The 18th century poet Edward Young warned, "Let no man trust the first false step of guilt; it hangs upon a precipice, whose steep descent in lost perdition ends."[23]

Surely the point is well established that there is a need in the human heart to acknowledge and confess our sin. The question then becomes, to whom do I make confession? Although there is one level on which the confession of sin is always appropriate, there are at least four levels on which confession is sometimes appropriate – the personal level, the private level, the priestly level, and the public level.

PERSONAL CONFESSION
(CONFESSION TO GOD)

Confession of sin on the personal level – man to God – is always appropriate because sin is always, first, and foremost against God. David wrote, "Against Thee, Thee only, I have sinned" (Psa. 51:4). Now it is true that he sinned against Uriah, against Bathsheba, and also against the people of Israel over whom he reigned. However, sin is not sin by definition unless it is against God.

The idea of confession is the admission of sin. "I confess" means I admit that this specific thing that I have or have not done is my responsibility. I agree with God that it is sin. The Greek word for confession means "to say the same things, to admit or declare oneself guilty of what one is accused."

But what is the purpose of confession? To answer that, we acknowledge that God has a tremendous desire, motivated by His love for man, TO FORGIVE. The whole plan of redemption laid down from the foundation of the world was for the purpose of making it possible for God to forgive man of his sins. The purpose of Calvary, the reason Christ became sin on our behalf (II Cor. 5:21) was so that a just God could count sinful man righteous, FORGIVEN!

Confession of sin is at the core of God's plan for forgiveness. In genuine conversion, there must be an acknowledgment of man's sinfulness and his need for a Savior. However, for the Christian, the confession of sin remains at the core of continual forgiveness. Thus the

Apostle John makes this powerful promise in I John 1:9, "If we confess our sins, He is faithful and righteous to forgive us our sins and to cleanse us from all unrighteousness."

WOW!!! God forgives! Confession makes application of the forgiveness appropriated for us when we received Christ as Lord and Savior. I don't free myself from sin by the admission of it. I can't break out of the prison of my sin by proclaiming it. Sin calls for forgiveness. Only God can forgive. Thus confession is directed to God who is merciful beyond comprehension and the forgiveness, the cleansing is accomplished by Him.

It is important to note that John said we are to confess our "sins," plural. As Christians, it is not our sinfulness but our specific sins that God wants us to confess. J. Oswald Sanders writes in *Prayer Power Unlimited*:

> There is a place for a general confession, for there are many sins of which we are unconscious or which we have overlooked; but this does not dispense with the necessity for a frank and full confession of specific sins. The confession should be made the moment we are conscious of having sinned, and not delayed until a more convenient time. We have the assurance that the moment we sincerely confess, that moment God freely forgives us and fellowship is restored.[24]

There is no comprehensive check list of sins for us to review in making confession to God. Don DeWelt, in his *Prayer Time: A Guide For Personal Worship*, has a section on confession for every day of the year. He lists at least 365 specific sins. However, that list is far from comprehensive. And it is good that there is no such list, for some people would surely abuse it by checking to make sure they hadn't missed committing any sins.

Basically there are three categories of sin of which man is guilty. There are sins of commission where we transgress God's law (I John 3:4). There are sins of omission when we fail to do that which God would have us do (James 4:17). Finally there are sins of the conscience when we go against that which we believe in our own heart to be right (Rom. 14:23). Suzannah Wesley's working definition of sin may be of some help.

> Whatever weakens your reason, impairs the tenderness of your conscience, obscures your sense of God, or takes away the relish for spiritual things; in short, whatever increases the strength and authority of your body over your mind – that thing is sin to you.[25]

Brethren, we need to be honest with ourselves and with God. Denial of sin only compounds it. Playing games with God fools no one but ourselves. I read of a little five-year old boy who got angry at his mother. He stomped off to his room where he packed his clothes in a paper sack. He would show her! He would run away! His mother, rather than object, helped him pack and then watched as he went out the front door and headed off down the street. Half an hour later the doorbell rang. When she opened the door, there stood the runaway, bedraggled, worried, and with reddened eyes wiped dry by his sleeve. In the most serious of tones he spoke, "Lady," he said, "somebody found your little boy."

People of all ages go to equally silly lengths to disguise or deny sin. God says, "Confess your sins and I will forgive." What parent among us will not deal more graciously with a child who sorrowfully acknowledges his disobedience than with the one who stubbornly refuses to acknowledge it?

Christian, develop the discipline of daily confessing your sins to God in prayer and of accepting His forgiveness. Without it, an insurmountable obstacle stands in the way of your spiritual growth.

Confessing sin against God is always appropriate. But are there times when confession needs to extend beyond that personal level? Yes, I believe there are.

PRIVATE CONFESSION
(CONFESSION TO THE OFFENDED)

The Bible makes it clear that if my sin has involved or offended another person that I must, when possible, go to that person and make confession to them as well. In His Sermon on the Mount, Jesus said:

> If therefore you are presenting your offering at the altar, and there remember that your brother has something against you, leave your offering there before the altar, and go your way, first be reconciled to your brother, and then come and present your offering (Matt. 5:23-24).

When sin is against God and God alone, then the confession need be made to no other. But when we have sinned against man as well as God, confession needs to be made to the offended party. When the prodigal son returned home, he confessed to his father, "I have sinned against heaven AND in your sight" (Luke 15:21). It is a humbling thing to have to go to your wife, or children, or co-workers, or friends and say, "I was wrong." But it is also essential to spiritual growth. Warren Myers says that a friend of his reminds each couple he counsels for marriage that "the seven hardest words in the English language are, `I was wrong, will you forgive me?' "[26]

Charles Keysor recounts this story from the book *Guilt & Freedom*:

> During a series of meetings with a group of pastors, a minister came and asked to see me privately. During our talk together he said, "I have something that's bothered me for years. When I was in seminary, I cheated on my final Greek exam. When I took the test I accidentally omitted one section of the translation. Since I usually did well in class, my professor called me at home to see what had happened. Since he trusted me a lot, he said, 'I'll let you translate the passage to me over the phone right now.'
>
> I told him all right, excused myself for a moment, and got both my Greek New Testament and an English translation. Then I translated it over the phone. But I was actually reading from the English. I got an A in the class and graduated from the seminary with honors, but I can't look that professor in the eye to this day. Every time I think about it, I feel like a hypocrite. I've prayed and prayed about it, but nothing seems to change."
>
> After talking over the situation, I suggested the only way to resolve the problem would be to telephone his professor and confess his cheating. He struggled with this for some minutes and finally said, "I just can't do it. What would he think of me?"
>
> I've never seen this pastor since, but I imagine he's still haunted by his guilt. His refusal to confess his cheating left him a victim of self-punishment.[27]

This man had four years of college and three years of seminary yet he didn't have enough common sense to see that his refusal to confess his sin to the person he had sinned against was a barricade to an effective prayer life and to further spiritual growth. His reputation and status in the church were more important to him than pleasing God. After all, if he called that professor and told him the truth, word might get around and might stand in the way of further professional success. Keysor suggests that his real problem was idolatry; for to consider anything more important than pleasing God is indeed to have an idol.

By the way, Matthew 18:15 makes it clear that if I am the offended party, the victim of another's sin, I have a responsibility to care enough for that individual to confront them about that sin. Jesus said I was first to do it in private, for the confession of sin or confrontation of sin ordinarily needs go no further than the parties immediately involved. There are yet to be mentioned two exceptions.

PRIESTLY CONFESSION
(CONFESSION TO A BROTHER OR SISTER)

I know that I run the risk of being misunderstood in using the term "priestly." Some will cite I Timothy 2:5 "There is one God, and one mediator also between God and men, the man Christ Jesus." I might be accused of suggesting the need for another mediator. Some might think I was advocating the sacrament of confession as practiced in Romanism where mere men claim the authority to absolve other men of sin. I am suggesting neither.

I am acknowledging the fact that ALL Christians are priests before God (I Peter 2:9) and that James exhorts us, "Therefore, confess your sins to one another, and pray for one another, so that you may be healed" (James 5:16). If I have confessed my sin to God and not gotten any peace; if I have gone to the offended party and privately acknowledged my sins and asked forgiveness and still not gotten any peace; it is most likely time to seek out a trusted brother or sister and practice James 5:16. That person may be one of the pastors on our staff. It may be your elder. It may be a close Christian friend with a good deal of spiritual maturity. But go, confess, and pray.

Bonhoeffer explains the value of priestly confession:

> A man who confesses his sins in the presence of a brother knows that he is no longer alone with himself; he experiences the presence of God in the reality of the other person. As long as I am by myself in the confession of my sins, everything remains in the dark, but in the presence of a brother, the sin has to be brought into the light.[28]

There simply must be this form of mutual ministry at work in the church. It is not something to be mandated or organized; but in practice, it is a sign of life and a miracle of grace. Martin Luther wrote:

> There is also a confession which may take place privately between two brothers and if, from some special cause, we become disturbed with restless anxiety and find our faith insufficient, we can make our complaint to a brother in this private confession and obtain his advice, comfort, and support whenever we desire. . . . Now wherever there is a heart which feels its sins and

desires consolation, it has here an unfailing resource in the Word of God, that God through a human being releases and acquits it of sin.[29]

Luther is not suggesting, nor am I suggesting that anyone other than Christ has the authority to forgive sins. The function of the brother or sister is to express and apply the Word of Christ which He has already spoken.

There is a secondary benefit to priestly confession which should also be mentioned. Walter Luthi points out that the process of confessing is significant and helpful in and of itself. Confessing calls for an examination of conscience and a deep evaluation of our spiritual life no matter what else takes place. "When one man opens his heart to another, that in itself means help, it means being lifted out of inward loneliness, out of ego-centricity, and out of a cramped state of mind."[30]

When seeking out someone with whom to share your confession, be careful and prayerful in your selection. Not all Christians are empathetic or understanding. Not all can keep a confidence. Not all can cope emotionally or spiritually with the knowledge of your sin. However, with the leading of the Spirit of God, priestly confession can produce powerful benefits for the child of God.

PUBLIC CONFESSION
(CONFESSION TO THE CHURCH)

The Matthew 18 passage referred to earlier, indicates that after dealing with an erring brother one-on-one and with two or three witnesses; if he does not repent, the matter is to be taken before the church (Matt. 18:17). While that passage deals with the disciplining of an erring brother, it would also seem to indicate that there are times when a person needs to publicly confess their sins. When the sin is public against the church, then the confession should be as public as the sin. When a person has spread lies, or has betrayed a trust of leadership, or used the church for selfish or immoral purposes, only public confession can correct the wrongs, restore confidence, and renew fellowship. The public nature of the confession will also no doubt discourage a repetition of the sin.

There does not appear to be Scriptural warrant or practical reason for confessing personal, secret sins publicly. Rather than a positive thing, I've seen much harm result for all involved. But our public sins need public confession.

CONCLUSION

Richard Foster makes this observation:

> The discipline of confession brings an end to pretense. God is calling into being a church that can openly confess its frail humanity and know the forgiving and empowering graces of Christ. Honesty leads to confession and confession leads to change. May God give grace to the church once again to recover the discipline of confession.[31]

Dawson Trotman, founder of the Navigators, spoke to a large conference of pastors and missionaries many years ago. Afterwards, one of his staff pointed out that he had made some very critical remarks about another Christian. The next day when he spoke, Trotman publicly asked forgiveness and in the process broke down in tears. Can you imagine what a humiliating situation that must have been? How could God use the message of a man who had been so public in his wrongdoing?

However, Trotman believed and practiced I John 1:9. He knew he was forgiven and that day he preached a message entitled, "The Need of the Hour." It was one of his most powerful and is still widely distributed today both in print and on tape.

So it can be with you. FORGIVEN! Free from guilt! No need for further remorse! You can be free of guilt, Christian, free by God's grace.

> If we confess our sins, He is faithful and righteous to forgive us our sins and to cleanse us from all unrighteousness (I John 1:9).
> How blessed is he whose transgression is forgiven, Whose sin is covered! How blessed is the man to whom the Lord does not impute iniquity, and in whose spirit there is no deceit! (Psa. 32:1-2).

THOUGHT QUESTIONS:

1. Why do you think David did not acknowledge his sin until confronted with it?

2. What are the consequences of unconfessed sin?

3. Can you think of problems in your own life which resulted from your refusal to acknowledge a certain sin in your life?

4. Why do you think God makes confession a condition of forgiveness?

5. Are your sins primarily ones of commission, omission, or conscience?

6. Can you think of instances when you've rationalized away your sin instead of dealing with it?

7. Can you think of specific instances when you've gone to a person you've sinned against and ask their forgiveness?

8. Who would you feel comfortable going to for priestly confession?

9. What benefits can you identify that would come from confessing your sins to a brother or sister in Christ?

10. When do you believe public confession would be appropriate?

11. Could the discipline of confession ever become an unhealthy preoccupation with sin? Can you think of examples?

12. Is there an obstacle to spiritual growth in your life that could be dealt with by the discipline of confession?

ASSIGNMENTS:

Read the following Biblical confessions of sin:

Genesis 41:9	Psalm 40:12
Genesis 44:16	Psalm 41:4
Exodus 9:27	Psalm 51:1
Exodus 10:16	Isaiah 6:5
I Samuel 15:24	Daniel 9:20

II Samuel 12:13	Matthew 27:4
II Samuel 24:10	Luke 5:8
I Chronicles 21:17	Luke 15:18
Psalm 32:5	Luke 18:13
Psalm 38:1-4	I Timothy 1:15

In David's prayer of confession in Psalm 51:1-17, he makes 17 requests of God. Read the passage, list his requests, and meditate on each one.

It is more difficult to confess some things than others. Thus we often leave certain problem areas of our lives not dealt with in confession.

Spend some quiet time with God this week and ask Him to bring to your mind those things that He knows you need to confess.

SCRIPTURE REFERENCES:

II Sam. 12:13	II Cor. 5:21	Luke 15:21
Exod. 20:12-14, 16-17	I John 1:9	Matt. 18:15-17
Psa. 51:1-17	I John 3:4	I Tim. 2:5
Psa. 32:1-5	James 4:17	I Pet. 2:9
Prov. 28:13	Rom. 14:23	James 5:16
Isa. 59:1-2	Matt. 5:23-24	

RECOMMENDED READING:

Come Clean by Charles Keysor
Confession & Forgiveness by Andrew Murray

Confess Your Sins by John R. Stott
Pray: How To Be Effective In Prayer by Warren Myers

A PRAYER OF CONFESSION:

"Blessed heavenly Father, I ask Your forgiveness for offending You by committing this sin of (name of the offense). I claim the cleansing that is mine through the blood of the Lord Jesus Christ. I address myself against Satan and all of his kingdom. I take away from you and all of your powers of darkness any ground you are claiming against me when I sinned in (name of offense). I claim that ground back in the name of the Lord Jesus Christ. I cover it with the blood of the Lord Jesus Christ and give all areas of my life over to the full control of the Holy Spirit."

–Mark Bubeck in THE ADVERSARY

QUOTABLE QUOTES:

"The confession of evil works is the first beginning of good works."

–Augustine of Hippo

"For a good confession, three things are necessary: an examination of conscience, sorrow, and a determination to avoid sin."

–St. Alphonsus Luguori

"Many Christians are unthinkably horrified when a real sinner is suddenly discovered among the righteous. So we remain alone with our sin, living in lies and hypocrisy. The fact is that we are sinners."

–Dietrich Bonhoeffer in LIFE TOGETHER

"If we confess our sins, He is faithful and righteous to forgive us our sins and to cleanse us from all unrighteousness."

–I John 1:9

"How blessed is he whose transgression is forgiven, whose sin is covered! How blessed is the man to whom the Lord does not impute iniquity, and in whose spirit there is no deceit!"

–Psalm 32:1-2

Chapter Four

GROWING THROUGH READING & WRITING

Peter writes, "Grow in the grace and knowledge of our Lord and Savior, Jesus Christ" (II Pet. 3:18). Paul writes in Romans 12:2, "Do not be conformed to this world, but be transformed by the renewing of your mind, that you may prove what the will of God is, that which is good and acceptable and perfect." But how do you grow spiritually; how do you renew your mind?

We're learning that there are many aids to spiritual growth that God has put at our disposal. We've already looked at prayer and the confession of sin as means to the end of spiritual growth. In the following chapters we'll look at Bible study, meditation, quiet time, fasting, personal worship, and service or ministry as disciplines leading to spiritual growth. All have strong, scriptural support for their practice. But now we turn our attention to what I want to call the new "3 R's" . . . "Reading, Riting, and Religion." I want to encourage you in the disciplines of reading for spiritual growth and of keeping a journal or prayer diary for the same purpose.

Let me quickly admit that I have very little Biblical authority for advocating either. I can assure you that the number of books you read or whether or not you keep a journal have no real bearing on your salvation but both can contribute significantly to your spiritual growth. While a strong case can be made for the importance of reading the Bible, I know of no verse of Scripture that requires you to read other books. And while we know that several of the apostles did a lot of writing, the only writing Jesus did which is mentioned in Scripture is whatever He wrote on the ground when the woman taken in adultery was brought to Him. That is hardly a Biblical mandate for journal keeping.

However, there is great practical value in both Christian reading and journaling for the purpose of spiritual growth. Thus it is altogether appropriate to include this chapter in this book.

The case can be made that most great Christian leaders of the ages have been well-read. It is also true that spiritual giants such as Augustine, John Wesley, George Whitefield, David Brainard, Francis Asbury, Andrew Murray, Oswald Chambers, C.S. Lewis, and Jim Elliott were journal-keepers, and we are all the richer for it. However, some people conclude that such disciplines are not for the "ordinary Christian." Richard Foster addresses that erroneous notion:

> We must not be led to believe that the Disciplines are for
> spiritual giants and hence beyond our reach, or for con-
> templatives who devote all their time to prayer and
> meditation. Far from it, God intends the disciplines of
> the spiritual life to be for ordinary human beings: peo-
> ple who have jobs, who care for children, who must
> wash dishes and mow lawns. In fact, the Disciplines are
> best exercised in the midst of our ordinary daily activi-
> ties.[32]

It is not my intention to lay a guilt trip on you just
because you don't keep a journal or haven't read a book
for your spiritual growth lately. If that were my purpose, I would have my work cut out for me for only
6.3% of the people surveyed kept a journal, only 20.2%
had ever kept a journal, and 41% of our people hadn't
read a single book to aid them in their spiritual growth
in the previous twelve months.

It is my intention to open your eyes to the exciting
disciplines of Christian reading and journal-keeping.
Hopefully, you will be motivated to take advantage of
these tremendously helpful tools for spiritual growth.

READING

Recently my wife Jan and I drove over to DePauw
University in Greencastle to hear my daughter Jennifer
play in the state music contest (where she got two supe-
rior ratings, by the way). Afterward, we stopped at the

Walden Inn to have lunch. A nice fire was roaring in the fireplace, and we stood close by to get warmed up from the frigid outside temperatures. We had been there before; but for the first time, I noticed the inscription on the fireplace mantle: "How many a man has dated a new era in his life from the reading of a book. –Henry David Thoreau, Reading, 1854."

That quotation really struck me because it has been true of my life. God has used people, events, classes, sermons, and various personal experiences to change my life. But as much as anything, He has used books. Significant changes have *often come in my life as a result of reading a book.*

Richard Foster relates this to the "renewing of the mind" to which Paul refers in Romans 12. "The mind is renewed by applying it to those things that will transform it."[33] Actually, this renewing of the mind can take place through all of the disciplines, and through the direct work of the Holy Spirit in the mind of the person who is yielded to and filled with Him. However, the discipline of reading has a direct impact. Remember the words of Paul in Philippians 4:8, "Finally, brethren, whatever is true, whatever is honorable, whatever is right, whatever is pure, whatever is lovely, whatever is of good repute, if there is any excellence and if anything worthy of praise, let your mind dwell on these things." Selective Christian reading allows us to "dwell on these things."

Topping our reading list should be the Bible, the very Word of God. The importance of reading, studying, meditating upon and even memorizing the Word of

God is stressed throughout Psalm 119. Listen to just this short section:

> How can a young man keep his way pure?
> By keeping it according to Thy Word.
> With all my heart I have sought Thee;
> Do not let me wander from Thy commandments.
> Thy word I have treasured in my heart,
> That I may not sin against Thee.
> Blessed art Thou, O Lord;
> Teach me Thy statutes.
> With my lips I have told of
> All the ordinances of Thy mouth.
> I have rejoiced in the way of Thy testimonies,
> As much as in all riches.
> I will meditate on Thy precepts,
> And regard Thy ways.
> I shall delight in Thy statutes;
> I shall not forget Thy word (vss. 9-16).

The reason for the importance of Scripture is clearly stated in II Timothy 3:16-17:

> All Scripture is inspired by God and profitable for teaching, for reproof, for correction, for training in righteousness; that the man of God may be adequate, equipped for every good work.

Not only will spiritual growth not take place apart from the Word, there can't even be spiritual birth apart from the Word. Paul tells us, "Faith comes by hearing and hearing by the word of Christ" (Rom. 10:17). Peter says, "You have been born again not of seed which is perishable but imperishable, that is, through the living and abiding word of God" (I Pet. 1:23). New Christians are told to "long for the pure milk of the word, that by it you may grow in respect to salvation" (I Pet. 2:2).

Although I personally do a good deal of Bible reading and study in sermon and lesson preparation, as a part of my personal, devotional life, I read a chapter from the Psalms, a chapter from Proverbs, and another section of Scripture each day. While I do not read the Bible through in its entirety every year, I do so every few years and urge you to do so from time to time as well. Several publishers now provide a "Through the Bible in a Year" arrangement of the Scripture in several versions. Old and New Testament sections are arranged thematically and dated so as to complete Genesis through Revelation in 365 days.

The fact is, however, most Christians spend little time really getting into the Word. Our spiritual disciplines survey revealed that less than half our people read God's Word as much as two or three times a week. Such neglect is not new. The Hebrew writer wrote in Hebrews 5:12, "For though by this time you ought to be teachers, you have need again for someone to teach you the elementary principles of the oracles of God, and you have come to need milk and not solid food."

As important as the reading of Scripture is, you will also find tremendous help in the devotional writings of others. The experiences of others in this pilgrimage we call the Christian life can provide encouragement, correction, illumination, instruction, counsel, and challenge. Many times my personal hunger for the experience of closeness to God comes from the words of trust, commitment, worship, and spiritual experience recorded by others.

Thus I make the reading of Christian devotional literature an important part of my daily quiet time. Currently I use a devotional guide that contains selections for meditation by various authors. In the past, I have used collections of essays by Christian authors like *The Joyful Christian* or *The Business Of Heaven* by C.S. Lewis; *The Martyred Christian* by Dietrich Bonhoeffer; or *Growing Strong In The Seasons Of Life* by Charles Swindoll. Other times I have simply read a chapter each day from a good book which has been recommended to me.

There are so many excellent, helpful books that I hardly know where to begin to recommend them to you. However, I went through all the correspondence I received from numerous Christian leaders across the nation in regard to the Christian disciplines and listed all the books they had mentioned. It was interesting to determine the most often mentioned. Out of hundreds recommended, the top ten were:

1. CELEBRATION OF DISCIPLINE by Richard Foster
2. ORDERING YOUR PRIVATE WORLD by Gordon MacDonald
3. THE PURSUIT OF HOLINESS by Jerry Bridges
4. THE IMITATION OF CHRIST by Thomas á Kempis
5. RESTORING YOUR SPIRITUAL PASSION by Gordon MacDonald
6. THE COST OF DISCIPLESHIP by Dietrich Bonhoeffer
7. THE PRACTICE OF GODLINESS by Jerry Bridges

8. AUTOBIOGRAPHY OF GEORGE MULLER
9. PRAYER POWER UNLIMITED by J. Oswald
   Sanders
10. MY UTMOST FOR HIS HIGHEST by Oswald
    Chambers

That really wouldn't be a bad reading list to start with. There are great Christian classics, books that have blessed Christians over the centuries, books like: *Confessions* by Augustine, *The Practice Of The Presence Of God* by Brother Lawrence, and *A Serious Call To A Devout & Holy Life* by William Law. There are inspirational books like: *Acres Of Diamonds* by Russell Conwell, *The Greatest Thing In The World* by Henry Drummond, *No Easy Road* by Dick Eastman, *A Taste Of New Wine* by Keith Miller, *The Christian's Secret Of A Happy Life* by Hannah Whitall Smith, or *The Pursuit Of God* By A.W. Tozer. And there are great works of Christian fiction and allegory like: *The Pilgrim's Progress* by John Bunyan, *Ruth* by Lois Henderson, *The Chronicles Of Narnia* (all seven volumes), and *The Screwtape Letters* by C.S. Lewis, and *In His Steps* by Charles Sheldon. Of course biographies are a great source of encouragement and a favorite of mine, but I won't even start naming them.

Suffice it to say that there are hundreds of books which would be of great value to you in your spiritual pilgrimage. But the sad truth is that in spite of availability and accessibility few Christians really practice the discipline of reading for growth. Only 8% of our members read more than 5 such books the previous year and 41% of our people didn't read a single book.

If that's true of you, you're missing out on so much. Several years ago I made a new year's resolution to read a book a week. Since then, circumstances haven't always allowed the completion of a book every week, but I've averaged nearly two. I'm not a speed reader in the technical sense although I have always read rather fast. Neither do I have a lot more free time than the average person. I work a 70+ hour week, zealously guard my time with my family, watch more ballgames than anyone probably should, teach seminary classes, thoroughly enjoy life, and still have time to read by making time. I often read a chapter in the morning after my devotions and before leaving for the office. I do most of my reading in the evening between 9:00 and 11:00. I also carry a book along with me for all those otherwise wasted times during the day like waiting for an appointment, waiting to be served in a restaurant, getting my hair cut, sitting in the dentist's chair, or even while tied up in a traffic jam.

You may never enjoy reading. But you can find time to practice the discipline of reading for spiritual growth if you will. Will you make such a commitment today? It's time for a visit to the library or the bookstore, or perhaps it's time just to get out that book you've been saying you were going to read.

The apostle Paul was sentenced to death and this execution was soon to take place. That makes it all the more significant that he wrote to Timothy, "When you come, bring . . . the books, especially the parchments" (II Tim. 4:13). To his dying day Paul was going to read, study, and learn.

WRITING

Let's turn our attention now to another discipline which complements reading, the keeping of a spiritual journal or prayer diary. Of all the disciplines mentioned on the survey, this is the least practiced as 93.7% did not keep a journal. I must also admit that it has been one of the most difficult disciplines for me to keep and I've been very spasmodic in practice over the years. However, I have always found it very rewarding after the fact. It is unfortunate that so many Christians have never even attempted it. Only 18% of the preachers surveyed kept a journal and only 40% have ever done so.

What are we really talking about? What is a journal? Here's one definition:

> A journal is a book in which you keep a personal record of events in your life, of your different relationships, of your response to things, of your feelings about things – of your search to find out who you are and what the meaning of your life might be. It is a book in which you carry out the greatest of life's adventures – the discovery of yourself.[34]

I like that. Ronald Klug in his excellent book on journaling, *How To Keep A Spiritual Journal*, offers this definition:

> A journal or diary (the terms are used interchangeably) is a day-book – a place to record daily happenings. But it is far more than that. A journal is also a tool for self-discovery, an aid to concentration, a mirror for the soul, a place to generate and capture ideas, a safety valve for emotions, a training ground for the writer, and a good friend and confidant.[35]

In keeping with that definition, Klug offers ten benefits of keeping a journal.[36] First, there is GROWTH IN
SELF-UNDERSTANDING. A spiritual journal gives you
a vehicle to examine your life, your faith, your feelings,
your relationships, and your goals. Next, it serves as
AN AID TO THE DEVOTIONAL LIFE. Susan Annette
Muto has written in that regard:

> Journaling is one of the most helpful exercises we can
> do to increase our capacity for meditation and prayer.
> Pausing daily or a few times a week to jot down our
> thoughts has a way of quieting and uncluttering our
> overactive, decentered lives. Writing helps us to work
> through detected obstacles to spiritual living ... A jour-
> nal is not only a record of events that touch and trans-
> form us; it is a private space in which we can meet our-
> selves in relation to others and to God.[37]

A third benefit of a journal is for GUIDANCE AND
DECISION-MAKING. The journal can be used for
debating the pros and cons of a decision. It also pro-
vides a record of the rationale for making the decision
and thus reenforces it. A fourth benefit is for MAKING
SENSE AND ORDER OF LIFE. Writing down thoughts
and feelings sorts out and clarifies them. Fifth, a journal
can be used for RELEASING EMOTIONS AND GAIN-
ING PERSPECTIVE. You can express joy, thanksgiving
and happiness. But a journal may be even more useful
as a means of espressing negative emotions. I've written
a lot of letters that were never sent because they went in
my journal. Do you want to tell someone off? Do it in
your journal. Madeleine L'Engle gives an excellent illustration of this benefit.

Not long ago, someone I love said something which wounded me grievously, and I was desolate that this person could have made such a comment to me. So, in great pain, I crawled to my journal and wrote it all out in a great burst of self-pity. And when I had set it down, when I had it before me, I saw that something I myself had said had called forth the words which had hurt me so. It had, in fact, been my own fault, but I would never have seen it if I had not written it out.[38]

Benefit number six is GREATER AWARENESS OF DAILY LIFE. You'll be more alert to what is going on around you and within you if you keep a journal. Seventh, there is SELF-EXPRESSION AND CREATIVITY. Eighth, there is a CLARIFYING OF BELIEFS. The very act of writing causes us to make more specific and clear our thoughts. Ninth, there is the benefit of SETTING GOALS AND MANAGING YOUR TIME. You can keep your goals before you in a journal and set your priorities for the best use of your time in reaching them. Then Klug's final benefit to journal-keeping is WORKING THROUGH PROBLEMS. Morton Kelsey observes very perceptively:

How much less powerful the emotions that consumed us on one day are when we look at them with a calmer disposition the next day. I have found that writing my fears down one by one can often remove the pain I feel when they are invading me like a hostile army. When we look at them lying helpless in black and white on the pages of our journal, they often assume their proper size.[39]

Karen Mains adds another important benefit of keeping a journal:

Journals give their owners A CONCRETE MEANS OF EVALUATING SPIRITUAL GROWTH. Reviewing our prayers is important. We see where we have been, how far we have come, and where it is we must go. Because journals can be reviewed from time to time, they provide a stabilizing influence. The long view of our spiritual development helps to keep us from becoming overwhelmed by our present failures or from becoming discouraged by today's painful circumstances.[40]

One final benefit of journaling is simply that it HELPS US TO REMEMBER. The Scriptures are filled with admonitions to remember. "Remember the former things long past" (Isa. 46:9). "Remember His wonderful deeds which He has done" (I Chron. 16:12). "Remember the former days" (Heb. 10:32). "Remember those who led you" (Heb. 13:7). And I get out my old journals and I REMEMBER.

Now, what should you write in a journal? Most basic of all, you can simply record events. There are many journals of great men of God that have been published. My favorite is John Wesley's. He often records the events of the day:

Tuesday, October 21, 1735 – (on a ship bound for America) – From four in the morning till five, each of us used private prayer. From five to seven we read the Bible together, carefully comparing it (that we might not lean to our own understandings) with the writing of the earliest ages. At seven we breakfasted. At eight were the public prayers. From nine to twelve I usually learned German, and Mr. Delamotte, Greek. My brother wrote sermons, and Mr. Ingham instructed the children. At twelve we met to give an account of one another ... About one we dined. The time from dinner to four we spent in reading ... At four were the evening

85

prayers . . . From five to six we again used private prayer. From six to seven, I read in my cabin to two or three of the passengers . . . At seven I joined with the Germans in their public services . . . At eight we met again to exhort and instruct one another. Between nine and ten, we went to bed, where neither the roaring of the sea nor the motion of the ship could take away the refreshing sleep which God gave us.[41]

Other times Wesley reflected on his reading:

Wednesday, July 19, 1749 – I finished the translation of MARTIN LUTHER'S LIFE. Doubtless he was a man highly favored of God and a blessed instrument in His hand. But oh! What a pity that he had no real faithful friend! None that would, at all hazards, rebuke him plainly and sharply, for his rough, untractable spirit, and bitter zeal for opinions, so greatly obstructive of the work of God![42]

Sometimes Wesley simply spoke his feelings!

Wednesday, January 16, 1760 – One came to me as she said, with a message from the Lord, to tell me that I was laying up treasures on earth, taking my ease, and minding only my eating and drinking. I told her God knew me better; and if He had sent her, He would have sent her with a more proper message.[43]

Other journal entries were reflective and full of thanksgiving:

Friday, June 28, 1782 – I entered into my eightieth year; but, blessed be God, my time is not `labor or sorrow.' I find no more pain or bodily infirmities than at five and twenty. This I still impute 1) to the power of God; 2) to my still traveling four or five thousand miles a year;

3) to my sleeping night or day, whenever I want it; 4) to my rising at a set hour; and 5) to my constant preaching, particularly in the morning.[44]

There are many other things you might want to write in your journal. You can record conversations, questions, memories, insights, achievements, failures, great world events, and quotations, letters, and even dreams.

You most certainly can write out prayers – prayers of praise, of confessions, of thanksgiving, or of petition. You can give testimony to answered prayer. You may want to reflect on your Bible reading or inspirational reading. Perhaps you'll want to write a spiritual biography. You see, there are few if any limits on what is appropriate.

There is no right or wrong way. Just get a blank book – bound, spiral, or loose leaf, set aside a time, and get started. However, Douglas Rumford, writing in the winter of 1982 issue of LEADERSHIP, offers these helpful principles. 1) Trust the Holy Spirit to guide you. Begin with prayer. 2) Work with feelings and perceptions. 3) Trust your own insights. Who besides the Holy Spirit is a better authority on you than you? 4) Be completely free. Write for your eyes only. Privacy should be preserved and respected. (5) Be honest. Say what you feel.[45]

It was also Douglas Rumford who wrote the following:

> One of the first instructions God gave to Moses after the Exodus was to "write these things in a book." Recalling the mighty acts of God was an essential element for sustaining the people's vision of God. What about our own "holy histories?" An invaluable tool for the preservation

of God's work and the application of His truth in our lives is a personal journal.[46]

CONCLUSION

"Reading, riting, and religion" – they do go hand in hand. Reading opens us to God's truth as expressed and revealed in so many ways. Writing opens us up before ourselves and God in a way that may otherwise be impossible. God wants that. He wants that personal, intimate, honest sharing. Why? Because He loves you. Jesus Christ, God's Son, cared so much for you that He gave His very life for you.

You can trust Him. You can share your innermost thoughts, motivations, and hurts with Him. That thought is captured in a great old hymn by Elisha Hoffman.

> I must tell Jesus all of my trials.
> I cannot bear these burdens alone,
> In my distress He kindly will help me;
> He ever loves and cares for His own.
> Tempted and tried, I need a great Savior,
> One who can help my burden to bear.
> I must tell Jesus, I must tell Jesus;
> He all my cares and sorrows will share.

THOUGHT QUESTIONS:

1. What book, outside the Bible, has made the greatest impact on your life?

2. What were your favorite childhood books and why?

3. Why do you (or why do you not) enjoy reading?

4. What is the greatest obstacle to your reading for spiritual growth? What can you do to overcome it?

5. What is the last book you read which really helped you spiritually? How did it help you?

6. Do you see reading as a legitimate Christian discipline? Why or why not? What do you intend to do about it? When?

7. Why do you think so few Christians maintain a journal?

8. After reading this chapter, how do you feel about journaling?

9. If you wanted to keep a journal, what do you think would be your greatest difficulty?

10. What do you believe would be the greatest benefit of journal-keeping?

ASSIGNMENTS:

If you are not currently reading a book for spiritual growth, choose one today and determine to read at least one chapter per day.

Set an attainable reading goal for the year.

Using the definition under Quotable Quotes as a thought starter, write out a journal entry for this day in your life.

Because keeping a journal is an exercise in self-discovery, try the following. As you look at the face of this clock, ask yourself, "What time is it in my life?" Let the question sink in. Then draw the hands on the clockface to indicate the time. Write a paragraph descriptive of your feelings.

SCRIPTURE REFERENCES:

II Peter 3:18   Rom. 10:17   Isa. 46:9
Rom. 12:2   I Peter 1:23, 2:2 I Chron. 16:12
Psalm 119:9-16   Heb. 5:12   Heb. 10:32, 13:7
II Tim. 3:16-17

RECOMMENDED READING:

Collections of Devotional Readings:
  The Business Of Heaven by C.S. Lewis
  The Martyred Christian by Dietrich Bonhoeffer
  Growing Strong In The Seasons Of Life by Charles
    Swindoll

Christian Classics:
  The Practice Of The Presence Of God by Brother
    Lawrence
  Confessions by Augustine
  A Serious Call To A Devout & Holy Life by William
    Law

Inspirational Books:
  The Cost Of Discipleship by Dietrich Bonhoeffer
  The Christian's Secret Of A Happy Life by Hannah
    Whitall Smith
  Acres Of Diamonds by Russell Conwell

Christian Allegory:
  The Pilgrims Progress by John Bunyan
  The Chronicles Of Narnia by C.S. Lewis
  The Singer by Calvin Miller

Christian Fiction:
  In His Steps by Charles Sheldon
  Ruth by Lois Henderson
  Christy by Catherine Marshall

Biographies – Historical:
  Here I Stand (Martin Luther) by Roland Bainton

The Life Of David Brainerd by Jonathan Edwards
George Muller Of Bristol by Arthur Pierson
Henry Martyn by Constance Padwick
The Life Of John Newton by Cecil Richard

Biographies – 20th Century:
    Born Again (Charles Colson) by Charles Colson
    Through Gates Of Splendor (Jim Elliot) by Elizabeth
        Elliot
    Surprised By Joy (C.S. Lewis) by C.S. Lewis
    The Hiding Place (Corrie ten Boom) by Corrie ten
        Boom

Journals:
    The Journal Of John Wesley
    George Whitefield's Journal
    The Genesee Diary (Henri Nouwen)
    The Life & Diary Of David Brainerd
    Livingstone's Private Journals
    Markings (Dag Hammarskgold)

Top Ten (from Christian Leaders' Survey):
1. *Celebration Of Discipline* by Richard Foster
2. *Ordering Your Private World* by Gordon MacDonald
3. *The Pursuit Of Holiness* by Jerry Bridges
4. *The Imitation Of Christ* by Thomas á Kempis
5. *Restoring Your Spiritual Passion* by Gordon
   MacDonald
6. *The Cost Of Discipleship* by Dietrich Bonhoeffer
7. *The Practice Of Godliness* by Jerry Bridges
8. *Autobiography Of George Muller*
9. *Prayer Power Unlimited* by J. Oswald Sanders

10. *My Utmost For His Highest* by Oswald Chambers

Books on Journaling:
  How To Keep A Spiritual Journal by Ronald Klug
  The Godhunt by David & Karen Mains
  Keeping Your Personal Journal by George F.
  Simons
  Keeping A Spiritual Journal by Harry Cargas &
  Roger Radley

QUOTABLE QUOTES:

"How many a man has dated a new era in his life from
the reading of a book."
                    –Henry David Thoreau, READING, 1854.

"A journal is a book in which you keep a personal
record of events in your life, of your different relationships, of your response to things, of your feelings about
things – of your search to find out who you are and
what the meaning of your life might be. It is a book in
which you carry out the greatest of life's adventures –
the discovery of yourself."
            –from KEEPING A SPIRITUAL JOURNAL by Cargas &
                                              Radley

Chapter Five

GROWING THROUGH BIBLE STUDY

The Bible is the most amazing book ever written. The writing was done by thirty to forty different men of many different occupations, living on three continents, in at least six countries. They wrote over a period of fifteen hundred years in three languages – Hebrew, Aramaic, and Greek. Yet the Bible has complete unity from beginning to end, is without contradiction, has one primary theme – God's redemptive plan for man, and one central figure – the Lord Jesus Christ. There is only one explanation for this. "All Scripture is inspired by God" (II Tim. 3:16). "Men moved by the Holy Spirit spoke from God" (II Pet. 1:21).

Henry H. Halley has written:

> Everybody ought to love the Bible. Everybody ought to
> read the Bible. Everybody. It is God's Word. It holds the
> solution of life. It tells about the best friend mankind
> ever had, the noblest, kindest, truest man that ever trod
> this earth.
>
> It is the most beautiful story ever told. It is the best
> guide to human conduct ever known. It gives a mean-
> ing, and a glow, and a joy, and a victory, and a destiny,
> and a glory, to life elsewhere unknown.
>
> There is nothing in history, or in literature, that in any
> wise compares with the simple annals of the Man of
> Galilee, who spent his days and nights ministering to
> the suffering, teaching human kindness, dying for
> human sin, rising to life that shall never end, and
> promising eternal security and eternal happiness to all
> who will come to Him.
>
> Most people, in their serious moods, must have some
> wonderment in their minds as to how things are going
> to stack up when the end comes. Laugh it off, toss it
> aside, as we may, THAT DAY WILL COME. And THEN
> WHAT? Well, it is the Bible that has the answer. And an
> unmistakable answer it is. There is a God. There is a
> heaven. There is a hell. There is a Saviour. There will be
> a day of judgment. Happy the man, who, in the days of
> his flesh, makes his peace with the Christ of the Bible,
> and gets himself ready for the final take-off.
>
> How can any thoughtful person keep his heart from
> warming up to Christ, and the Book that tells about
> Him? Everybody ought to love the Bible. Everybody.
> EVERYBODY.[47]

The Psalmist certainly had learned the importance
and benefit of spending time in the Word of God:

O how I love Thy Law!
It is my meditation all the day.
Thy commandments make me wiser than my enemies,

For they are ever mine.
I have more insight than all my teachers,
For Thy testimonies are my meditation.
I understand more than the aged,
Because I have observed Thy precepts.
I have restrained my feet from every evil way,
That I may keep Thy word.
I have not turned aside from Thine ordinances,
For Thou Thyself hast taught me.
How sweet are Thy words to my taste!
Yes, sweeter than honey to my mouth!
From Thy precepts I get understanding;
Therefore I hate every false way (Psa. 119:97-104).

Great men through the years have attested to the importance of God's Word in their lives. Listen to just a few:

Abraham Lincoln: "I believe the Bible is the best gift God has ever given to man. All the good from the Savior of the world is communicated to us through this Book."

Horace Greeley: "It is impossible to enslave mentally or socially a Bible-reading people. The principles of the Bible are the groundwork of human freedom."

Patrick Henry: "The Bible is worth all other books which have ever been printed."

Robert E. Lee: "In all my perplexities and distresses, the Bible has never failed to give me light and strength."

Napoleon Bonaparte: "The Bible is no mere book, but a living creature, with a power that conquers all who oppose it."

John Quincy Adams: "So great is my veneration for the Bible that the earlier my children begin to read it, the more confident will be my hope that they will prove useful citizens of their country and respectable members of society. I have for many years made it a practice to read through the Bible once every year."

Charles Dickens: "The New Testament is the very best book that ever was or ever will be known in the world."

W.E. Gladstone: "I have known ninety-five of the world's

great men in my time, and of these, eighty-seven were follow-
ers of the Bible. The Bible is stamped with a specialty of signs,
and an immeasurable distance separates it from all competi-
tors."[48]

Now all these testimonies and thousands like them
underscore the importance of the Bible. However, they
do us no good unless we read, meditate upon, and
incorporate into our own lives that which is the very
Word of God. Bible study and prayer stand side by side
as the primary means of spiritual growth in a Christian's life. Yet the truth is that a minority of Christians
do any serious Bible study. There is a growing awareness of need. There is evidence of hunger. But by their
own admission 54% of the people surveyed didn't even
read the Bible more than once a week, let alone really
study God's Word.

Many believers are suffering serious spiritual anemia.
But it is no wonder. Scripture is the food of the soul. The
Bible identifies it as milk, meat, and bread. No one
among us could survive physically on a a little milk
once a week. Yet many are trying to survive spiritually
on that basis. Don't you see how foolish that is? It is
time for a return to the discipline of Bible study for spiritual growth.

Andrew Murray has a chapter called "Feeding on the
Word" in his book, THE INNER LIFE.[49] He bases it on
Jeremiah 15:16 where Jeremiah prays, "Thy words were
found and I ate them, and Thy words became for me a
joy and the delight of my heart." Three concepts are
suggested in that verse. Murray refers to finding, eating,
and rejoicing. However, I'd like to redefine those con-

cepts using the words discover, digest, and delight.

DISCOVER

You need to DISCOVER that the Bible is an open, exciting, rewarding book whose truths are more valuable than gold. There is only one way to do that and that is to get into the Word for yourself.

First, we must take time. Surely fifteen or twenty minutes a day to read and reflect on the Word is not unreasonable for the busiest of people. However, I'd like to suggest that you set aside a time at least once a week for extended Bible study. We find time to eat, sleep, bathe, and work. Most of us spend hours in front of the TV or playing games. Find time to study no matter whatever else you have to drop. National Geographic magazine relates a touching story about eighty-one year old Carl Sharmith, a veteran park ranger in Yosemite National Park. He was at his tent trying to rest after another long hot day of work. His face was peeling from his sunburn; and his eyes were watery, partly from age and fatigue, but partly from the hurt he felt after once again hearing an old, old question. It was a lady tourist who had approached him and said, "I've only got an hour to spend at Yosemite. What should I do? Where should I go?" When he was able to reply the old ranger said, "Ah, lady. Only an hour. I suppose if I had only one hour to spend at Yosemite, I'd just walk over there by the river and sit down and cry."[50] Our desire for discovery of God's Word should make Bible study a priority in our lives, causing us to make time.

When the best time is depends on you. Choose the time of day when you are most alert, wide awake, unrushed, and can really concentrate. For most people, that will be early morning. But for some it will be late evening or some other time of the day. Whatever time it is, be consistent. Consistency is the key to building a devotional life in all its elements.

Secondly, use a plan. I would strongly encourage the use of a devotional study guide. One of the best is *This Morning With God*, edited by Carol Adeney and published by InterVarsity. It will take you through an inductive study of the entire Bible in just four years using probing questions on every passage. If your initial desire is simply to read through the Bible, there are many reading schedules available. There are 1189 chapters in the Bible. Thus, if you read three chapters a day, five days a week, and four chapters on Saturday and Sunday, you'll finish in a year. If you do that, let me urge you not to read straight through from Genesis to Revelation but to intersperse your reading of the Old Testament with the reading of the New Testament.

Knofel Staton of Pacific Christian College recommends the following. Read one chapter of Proverbs every day corresponding to the day of the month. Read one Psalm each day. Divide the rest of the pages in the Old Testament by 180 and read that many pages a day (you would read the Old Testament twice each year). Divide the pages of the New Testament by ninety and read that many pages each day (you would read the New Testament through every three months).[51]

Again, the plan itself is not as important as that you

have a plan. Habitual, systematic study is what counts. Occasional or spasmodic study is like occasional physical exercise. It does very little good. Develop a system and follow it. Our inner life needs regular, daily food.

On this journey of discovery, it is also very important that you understand the goal. Bible study is not in itself a virtue. There are people who study the Bible with all sorts of intentions, many of which do not honor nor glorify the Lord. The primary reason to discover the Word of God is to be transformed into the image of God's Son, Jesus Christ. God wants you to be saved and to grow to be more and more like Jesus. Paul wrote in Romans 8:29, "Whom [God] foreknew, He also predestined to become conformed to the image of His Son." Study of God's Word is essential to that process.

Finally, if we are going to discover God's Word, we need to make personal preparations even as explorers, ancient and modern, have done before setting out on an expedition. Personal preparations for the Christian start with a CLEANSED LIFE (I John 1:9). Unconfessed sin will make us blind to important teachings of God's Word. WE NEED TO PRAY FOR UNDERSTANDING. The Psalmist prayed, "Open my eyes, that I may behold wonderful things from thy law" (Psa. 119:18). THERE SHOULD BE A DEPENDENCY ON THE HOLY SPIRIT AS OUR GUIDE in this journey of discovery. Paul reminds us in I Corinthians 2:12, "Now we have received, not the spirit of the world, but the Spirit who is from God, that we might know the things freely given to us by God." Furthermore, personal preparation involves A WILLINGNESS TO OBEY. Jesus made this very significant statement in John 7:17, "If any man is willing to do His will, he shall know of the teaching whether it is of God, or whether I speak from Myself." We can discover God's will only as we are willing to respond to it.

Frank Gaebelein is a great educator who has been at the forefront of the Christian school movement for many years. When asked what counsel he would want to offer to future generations of Christians, he responded, "Maintain at all costs a daily time of Scripture reading and prayer. As I look back, I see that the most formative influence in my life and thought has been my daily contact with Scripture over 60 years."[52] He had learned the importance of discovering the Word.

DIGEST

It is not enough to merely discover or encounter God's Word; we must take it into and make it a part of our lives. Jeremiah said, "Thy words were found and I ATE them." Here's where the dynamics of study come into play. There are many approaches to Bible study: analytical verse-by-verse, inductive, topical, character study, informational, and so forth.

All forms of Bible study have their own unique values and all can contribute to Christian growth. However, my primary concern here is with devotional study of the Word. Whatever other forms of study you adopt, do practice this one. James pictures the Word of God as being like a mirror which reveals what we look like to God (James 1:23-25). The Navigator's *Bible Study Hand-*

book suggests the acrostic SPECK to represent five things we can look for in such a study. Is there a SIN for me to avoid? Is there a PROMISE from God for me to claim? Is there an EXAMPLE for me to follow? Is there a COMMAND for me to obey? How can this passage increase my KNOWLEDGE about God or His Son? Other questions you might ask are: Is there a warning for me to heed? Is there some encouragement I can use? Are these words of praise I can repeat? Is there an experience described that has been my experience?[53]

Notice that the focal point of devotional study is YOU. It is for your spiritual help, correction, instruction, growth, and inspiration. The question to be answered again and again is, How does this relate to ME? This isn't selfish. It is the reason God gave us His Word.

It is not our purpose here to go into any sort of detailed instruction on the methodology of Bible study. Irving Jensen has an excellent chapter on "The Activities of Devotional Reading" in his book *How To Profit From Bible Reading*. Other good resources are listed at the end of this chapter.

However, it is important to remember that in any kind of Bible study there are three important elements. First there is OBSERVATION. We must determine what the text actually says. This requires careful attention to that which we're reading. It also requires a mind that is open even to that which differs from our preconceived notions. A good modern translation is a tremendous aid to observation. I would recommend either the New American Standard Bible or the New International Version.

After observation comes INTERPRETATION. In this step, we must determine the author's meaning. What was the Holy Spirit trying to say through the writer in this passage? Remember, words change. Cultures change. But our concern is what was meant by the author? How was the passage understood by its original readers?

Finally, there must be APPLICATION. How does this apply to me? Observation and interpretation are useless if we don't make personal application. The Psalmist said, "I have considered my ways, and turned my feet to Thy testimonies. I hastened and did not delay to keep Thy commandments" (Psa. 119:59-60). That's what God wants you and me to do. Study in and of itself has no merit unless it results in changed lives. Listen to James:

> But prove yourselves doers of the word, and not merely hearers who delude themselves. For if any one is a hearer of the word and not a doer, he is like a man who looks at his natural face in a mirror; for once he has looked at himself and gone away, he has immediately forgotten what kind of person he was. But one who looks intently at the perfect law, the law of liberty and abides by it, not having become a forgetful hearer but an effectual doer, this man shall be blessed in what he does (James 1:22-25).

DELIGHT

Jeremiah said, "Thy words were found and I ate them, and thy words became for me a joy and the delight of my heart." David wrote, "How blessed is the man who does not walk in the counsel of the wicked, nor stand in the path of sinners, nor sit in the seat of scoffers! But his delight is in the law of the Lord!" (Psa. 1:1-2) What are the benefits of Bible study that bring such delight? There are many but let me mention a few.

The Bible gives life. Paul wrote to Timothy, "From childhood you have known the sacred writings which are able to give you wisdom that leads to salvation through faith which is in Christ Jesus" (II Tim. 3:15). Not only is the Word of God used of the Spirit of God in the new birth (I Pet. 1:23), but having been born again, it is the food by which life is sustained (I Peter 2:2). Jesus said, "Man shall not live on bread alone, but on every word that proceeds out of the mouth of God" (Matt. 4:4). Strong truth makes strong Christians stronger. Billy Graham said:

> Through the years of experience I have learned that it is far better to miss breakfast than to forego a session with His Word. Not that the Bible is some sort of religious fetish which brings good fortune, but that I myself lack decisiveness and purpose and guidance when I neglect what is more important than my necessary food.[54]

Secondly, the Bible guides. It gives us moral guidance. "How can a young man keep his way pure? By keeping it according to Thy word" (Psa. 119:9). It also gives us guidance through the confusion of life. "Thy word is a lamp to my feet and a light to my path" (Psa. 119:105).

The Bible liberates. It not only reveals God's standards but sets us free to keep them. "Thy word I have treasured in my heart, that I may not sin against Thee," said the Psalmist (119:11). Jesus said, "You shall know the truth, and the truth shall make you free" (John 8:32).

There are many other benefits which bring delight in Psalm 119. The Bible gives wisdom. "I have more insight than all my teachers, for Thy testimonies are my meditation. I understand more than the aged because I have observed thy precepts" (vs. 99-100). The Bible gives peace. "Those who love Thy law have great peace" (vs. 165).

Furthermore, the Bible instructs. "Whatever was written in earlier times was written for our instruction, that through perseverance and the encouragement of the Scriptures we might have hope" (Rom. 15:4). Jesus said, "the Scriptures . . . bear witness of me" (John 5:39). Paul said, "All Scripture is . . . profitable for teaching" (II Tim. 3:16).

Finally, the Bible influences. It is not static. It condones or condemns, it illuminates or incinerates, but it is never unproductive. It is the "power of God," (Rom. 1:16) "the sword of the Spirit," (Eph. 6:17) the divider "of soul and spirit, of both joint and marrow, and able to judge the thoughts and intentions of the heart" (Heb. 4:12).

Is it any wonder that discovery and digesting of the Word should lead to delight? Among the responses to the Spiritual Disciplines survey distributed to ministers was this statement, "I still have a long way to go. But prayer, meditation, and Bible reading are indispensible. If I skip them, it is as though I have missed a meal. I AM ADDICTED TO GOD!" Praise the Lord! Don't you want to be addicted to God?

CONCLUSION

From the pen of A.F. Miller come these words:

The Bible reveals the mind of God, the state of man, the way of salvation, the doom of sinners, the happiness of believers. Its doctrines are holy, its precepts binding, its histories true, its decisions immutable.

It contains light to direct you, food to support you, comfort to cheer you. It should fill the memory, rule the heart, guide the feet. It is a mine of wealth, a paradise of glory, a river of pleasure.

Here paradise is restored, heaven is opened, hell is disclosed. Christ is its grand object, our good its design, the glory of God its end.

It is given you in life, will be opened in judgment and remembered forever. It rebukes the slightest sin, woos the greatest sinner, wins the hardest heart.

It offers protection in infancy, happiness in childhood, inspiration in youth, strength for maturity, assurance for old age, comfort in death, and salvation and riches, glory and reward for all eternity.[55]

Now, all of that is true, but let me be quick to add that it is not the Bible we worship. The Bible, God's written Word, is designed to point us to Christ, the Living Word. Apart from Him, the Bible loses its worth. Our aim is not to know the Bible but to know Christ. John White has correctly stated:

Knowledge, especially biblical knowledge, has the same effect as wine when it goes to your head. You become dizzily exalted. But Bible study should be done not with a view to knowing ABOUT Christ, but knowing HIM personally.[56]

The song writer puts it in proper perspective:

Beyond the sacred page
I seek thee, Lord.
My spirit pants for Thee,
O Living Word.

Oswald J. Smith was the founding pastor of The Peoples Church in Toronto. Some years ago he wrote:

You tell me that the Bible is dry and uninteresting, and that that is why you do not read it. May I say that the reason you find it dry and uninteresting is because you do not know the Author. You may have met the Author, but you have not become acquainted with Him. Once you really know Him, you will enjoy everything that has come from Him.

There was one time a young woman who tried to read a book of poems. She found them so dry and uninteresting, however, that she threw them aside. Later on she met the young man who had written them and fell in love with him. Then once again she picked up the book of poems, and this time, to her utter amazement and astonishment, she found them the most interesting poems she had ever read in her life. What made the difference? They were still the same poems they had been before. The difference was in her, not in the poems. She had now met the author, and as she read them she thought of him.

So will it be with you. If you know the Author, the Lord Jesus Christ, you will revel in His Word. It will mean more to you than any other book. The more you read it, the more you will want to read it.[57]

THOUGHT QUESTIONS:

1. What is the most amazing thing about the Bible to you?
2. Why do you believe there are so many Christians who do so little Bible study?

3. Evaluate your own practice of Bible study. Are you pleased? If not, why do you not study the Bible more?

4. Is time a factor? Evaluate your schedule. How much time do you spend watching TV, reading the newspaper or magazines, in recreation or hobbies?

5. If you were to seriously practice the discipline of Bible study, when would be the best time? How could you arrange that?

6. Have you ever read the Bible in its entirety? Will you?

7. What do you understand the goal or purpose of Bible study to be?

8. In what ways is the Bible like a mirror (James 1:23-25)?

9. What are some of the questions we should ask concerning a text when studying devotionally?

10. Do you remember the three main elements of Bible study from this chapter? What are they and what do they mean?

11. In your opinion, what are the greatest benefits to be derived from Bible study?

12. In what ways would spending more time in study of God's Word impact on your relationship with Him?

ASSIGNMENTS:

Read Psalm 119.

Read a favorite passage of Scripture. Now, list any SINS to be avoided, PROMISES to be claimed, EXAMPLES to be followed, COMMANDS to be obeyed, KNOWLEDGE to be added, WARNINGS to be heeded,

ENCOURAGEMENT to be used, PRAISE to be repeated, and/or EXPERIENCES to be identified with.

SCRIPTURE REFERENCES:

II Timothy 3:14-17	John 7:17	Psalm 119:105,11
II Peter 1:19-21	James 1:23-25	John 8:32
Psalm 119:97-104	Psalm 119:59-60	Psalm 119:165
Jeremiah 15:16	Psalm 1:1-2	Romans 15:4
Romans 8:29	I Peter 1:23	John 5:39
I John 1:9	I Peter 2:2	Romans 1:16
Psalm 119:18	Matthew 4:4	Ephesians 6:17
I Corinthians 2:12	Psalm 119:9	Hebrews 4:12

RECOMMENDED READING:

How To Profit From Bible Reading by Irving L. Jensen

How To Read The Bible For All It's Worth by Gordon Fee & Douglas Stuart

How To Read The Bible by A.J. Conyers

The Navigator Bible Studies Handbook

Selecting A Translation Of The Bible by Lewis Foster

This Morning With God edited by Carol Adeney

CHOOSING A TRANSLATION:

It is good to regularly read from a good, literal translation of the Bible. However, it is also good to read the same passage from a freer translation to aid your understanding. Here are the major, modern English versions ranked from most literal to freer translations to paraphrases.

1. New King James Version (NKJV, 1982)
2. New American Standard Bible (NASB, 1971)
3. Revised Standard Version (RSV, 1952)
4. New Berkeley Version in Modern English (MLB, 1954)
5. New International Version (NIV, 1978)
6. Good News Bible (TEV, 1976)
7. New English Bible (NEB, 1970)
8. Jerusalem Bible (JB, 1966)
9. New Testament in Modern English (Phillips, 1958)
10. The Living Bible (TLB, 1971)

QUOTABLE QUOTES:

"I am a Bible bigot. I follow it in all things, both great and small."

–John Wesley in his *Journal*

"When you have read the Bible, you will know it is the Word of God, because you will have found it the key to your own heart, your own happiness, and you own duty."

–Woodrow Wilson

"The reason people are down on the Bible is because they are not up on the Bible."

–W.W. Ayer

"If there is anything in my thoughts or style to commend, the credit is due to my parents for instilling in me an early love of the Scriptures."

–Daniel Webster

Chapter Six

GROWING THROUGH MEDITATION

Have you ever wished for a thirty-hour day? Surely this extra time would relieve the tremendous pressure under which we live. Our lives leave a trail of unfinished tasks. Unanswered letters, unvisited friends, unwritten articles, and unread books haunt quiet moments when we stop to evaluate. We desperately need relief.

But would a thirty-hour day really solve the problem? Wouldn't we soon be just as frustrated as we are now with our twenty-four allotment? A mother's work is never finished, and neither is that of any student, teacher, minister, or anyone else we know. Nor will the passage of time help us catch up. Children grow in number and age to require more of our time. Greater experience in profession and church brings more exacting assignments. So we find ourselves working more and enjoying it less.[58]

Those insightful words from the opening paragraphs of Charles Hummel's powerful essay, "Tyranny of the Urgent," are certainly reflective of much of my life. How about you? A verse that rebukes me each time I read it is Psalm 46:10, "Be still and know that I am God." I don't do that very well. And I'm not alone. It was no surprise in the Spiritual Disciplines Survey to find that the number one enemy of a strong, personal devotional life is busyness. But Hummel is right when he goes on to observe:

> Prayerful waiting on God is indispensable to effective service. Like the time-out in a football game, it enables us to catch our breath and fix new strategy. As we wait for directives, the Lord frees us from the tyranny of the urgent. He shows us the truth about Himself, ourselves, and our tasks. He impresses on our minds the assignments He wants us to undertake.

Our topic is "Growing Through Meditation." But in reality, before we can even think about meditation, we have to learn about solitude and silence. We need a return in our lives to the discipline of quiet, solitude, contemplation, and meditation. However, the truth is that such disciplines go against the flow of our culture and are conspicuously absent from most of our lives. Jean Fleming has written an excellent book on this very problem titled, *Between Walden & The Whirlwind*. In it she rightly states, "Our practical, materialistic society so values action over meditation, study and prayer that we often feel guilty when we stop to think, study, or pray."[59] I can identify with that, can't you?

Further compounding the problem is the attitude of

many Christians toward the whole concept of meditation. One Sunday I read a quote on meditation by Richard Foster. A very agitated lady met me at the door and was quick to point out that "meditation is of the devil." As with many other Christians, she reacted to the word by thinking of Eastern mysticism, Transcendental Meditation, Zen or Yoga. Actually the emphases on these things in our culture is in part reflective of the default of the church in the area of Biblical meditation. It is certainly a sad state of affairs when we have so long neglected a Biblical, spiritual discipline that we believe it to be of the devil.

Tilden Edwards tells of an instructor in a Christian high school who decided to introduce the discipline of meditation to his students. Week by week the time was increased to a maximum of ten minutes. The response of the students was dramatic. One boy spoke for most in the class when he said, "It is the only time in my day when I am not expected to achieve something." However, the parental response, while equally dramatic, was quite different, "It isn't Christian," said one. "I'm not paying all that tuition for my child to sit there and do nothing," said another.[60] Isn't it strange that ten minutes of silence and meditation would be so threatening to Christians?

I say all of that to acknowledge that some of you most likely have some built-in hangups and reservations. But this chapter is for Christians in a whirlwind culture striving to live Christlike lives. In the midst of our chaotic lives of activities, demands and responsibilities, it is possible to retreat, reflect and react and by so doing to feed the inner man, to grow in our spiritual lives, while remaining intensely involved in a very needy world.

RETREAT

First, we must retreat from that world, and seek solitude and quiet. And while solitude does not necessarily mean retreating physically from people and the world's activities, there is often that need as we see in the example of Jesus. At the beginning of His ministry, Jesus spent forty days alone in the wilderness. The night before He chose His disciples, He spent the entire night alone with His Father. When he heard of the death of John the Baptist, Matthew observes, "He withdrew from there in a boat, to a lonely place by Himself" (Matt. 14:13). After the feeding of the five thousand, Jesus sent the disciples away so He could be alone. After the twelve had returned from their mission of healing and preaching, Jesus said to them, "Come away by yourselves to a lonely place and rest for awhile" (Mark 6:31). The examples are too numerous to mention them all. But remember when His mission was on the line, His purpose for coming, Jesus withdrew to pray in the Garden of Gethsemane. Jesus needed and sought solitude.

Why, then, is modern-day man so resistant to solitude and so afraid of silence? We surround ourselves with noise through all our waking hours. Why? I believe Susan Annette Muto is right on target when she writes:

A common problem, related to why we may seek to

escape silence, is the discovery that it evokes nameless misgivings, guilt feelings, strange, disquieting anxiety. Anything is better than this mess, and so we flick on the radio or pick up the phone and talk to a friend. If we can pass through these initial fears and remain silent, we may experience a gradual waning of inner chaos. Silence becomes like a creative space in which we regain perspective on the whole.[61]

Some people would lament the lack of opportunity for solitude. I honestly believe all of us have the opportunity but we're afraid of it. Only a recognition of the desperate need we have in this area will enable us to overcome our fears. Preachers, myself included, are notoriously bad about comparing hectic schedules as though the busier our lives, the more spiritual we are. We even admire and give praise to our brothers and sisters in Christ who pack a maximum of activities into their week. Perhaps we need to slow down at least long enough to ask ourselves, "Just why are you doing this?" Certainly the Bible calls upon us to give careful thought to the use of our time. Paul writes, "Be careful how you walk, not as unwise men but as wise, making the most of your time because the days are evil. So then do not be foolish, but understand what the will of the Lord is" (Eph. 5:15-17).

Pastor, professor, and theologian Henri Nouwen has addressed our need for solitude in his book, *Making All Things New*. He writes:

Without solitude it is virtually impossible to live a spiritual life. Solitude begins with a time and place for God and for Him alone. If we really believe not only that God exists but also that He is actively present in our lives—healing, teaching, and guiding—we need to set aside a time and space to give Him our undivided attention. Jesus says, 'Go to your private room and, when you have shut your door, pray to your father who is in that secret place.' (Matt. 6:6)[62]

Morton Kelsey underlines the need for solitude:

As long as my mind is raging with thoughts, ideas, plans, and fears, I cannot listen significantly to God or any other dimension of reality.[63]

Dietrich Bonhoeffer adds his endorsement in *Life Together*:

As there are definite hours in the Christian's day for the Word, particularly the time of common worship and prayer, so the day also needs definite times of silence, silence under the Word and silence that comes out of the Word.[64]

I can only say that as I grow older and hopefully more mature in my Christian walk, I need silence, I need time alone with God. Satan, my personality, my lifestyle and the demands of my ministry all work against it. But I have that need. I've always had the need. I just didn't recognize it. However, now I have that hunger in my heart. Francois Fenelon said:

Be silent, and listen to God. Let your heart be in such a state of preparation that His Spirit may impress upon you such virtues as will please Him. Let all that is within you listen to Him. This silence of all outward and earthly affection and of human thought within us is essential if we are to hear His voice.[65]

Now, how can we achieve such solitude in the midst of our busy lives? Henri Nouwen, the theologian I mentioned earlier, took seven months away from his teaching duties at Yale Divinity School and spent them in a Trappist Monastery in upstate New York. His record of that experience, *The Genesee Diary*, certainly blessed my life even as the experience was life changing for him. But let's face it; that is completely out of the question for most of us and few of us would be prepared to benefit all that much from it anyway.

The truth is that you don't have to go to a monastery or even leave your everyday world to find solitude. There are monasteries, deserts or wildernesses of solitude already in our lives if we would only recognize and appreciate them. What about the drive to work in the morning? Before that, what about those first moments of wakefulness while you're still in bed, before the rest of the family is up? There is the solitude of that first cup of coffee while looking out the window at the dawning of a new day. There can be moments of solitude for the housewife while ironing or vacuuming. There can be moments of solitude for the business executive while waiting for the next appointment or for the factory worker finding a place by himself during break time. I often stop in the hospital chapel for a few moments of solitude when I'm calling there.

Those moments are there if we'll look for them. Richard Foster told of driving a load of chattering kids and adults to the airport. "Let's play a game," he said, "and see if we can be absolutely quiet until we reach the airport (about five minutes away)." It worked beautifully. When I return home late in the evening, especially on a bright, starry, moonlit night, I often just stand in my backyard and gaze into the heavens and experience the solitude God has so graciously provided.

What else can you do? Develop your own quiet place at home. For me it is a certain chair in our family room. Maybe your quiet place will be a certain room, maybe a large closet, perhaps a park in the spring and summer, or maybe it will be the prayer chapel at church.

Perhaps from time to time you could take a whole day to go away to a state park and just spend some time alone with God. When on vacation, I often go off alone to spend some quiet time alone with the Lord in the midst of His beautiful creation. Mountains, oceans, lakes, rivers, plains, and forests all have their special contribution to make to time spent alone with their Creator. Don't you want that? Doesn't that excite you? Don't you hunger for a greater experience of closeness to the Lord? It is there but our hearts, minds, and souls must be attuned to the solitude God has already provided.

REFLECT

Solitude is enjoyable in itself. It is beneficial in that it allows us to listen to God if we will. However, solitude is especially important as it relates to meditation; and meditation from a Biblical perspective is simply the conscious, intelligent reflection of the mind on spiritual truth. Lynne Hybels in her excellent book, *The Joy Of*

Personal Worship, points out that meditation "implies the conscious, intelligent use of the mind. It is not a meaningless repetition of words as encouraged in Eastern thought or forbidden in Scripture ('do not use meaningless repetition')."[66] The dictionary definition of meditate is, "to focus one's thoughts on, to reflect or ponder over." Again, from a Biblical standpoint, it is the concentration of the soul on the things of God.

Is there Biblical precedent or mandate? Listen to God's command to Joshua:

> This book of the law shall not depart from your mouth, but you shall meditate on it day and night, so that you may be careful to do according to all that is written in it; for then you will make your way prosperous, and then you will have success (Josh. 1:8).

One of the most beautiful prayers in the Bible is found in Psalm 19:14:

> Let the words of my mouth and the meditation of my heart be acceptable in Thy sight, O Lord, my rock and my redeemer.

God's blessings are often promised to those who meditate as in Psalm 1:1-2:

> How blessed is the man who does not walk in the counsel of the wicked, nor stand in the path of sinners, nor sit in the seat of scoffers! But his delight is in the law of the Lord. And in His law he meditates day and night.

Understanding what meditation is and that it is a Biblical discipline, the important question becomes one of what the subject of such reflection is to be. We get some guidance as to the answer in Colossians 3:1-2:

> If then you have been raised up with Christ, keep seeking the things above, where Christ is, seated at the right hand of God. Set your mind on the things above, not on the things that are on earth.

First, we can meditate on God Himself.

> When I remember Thee on my bed, I meditate on Thee in the night watches. For Thou hast been my help, and in the shadow of Thy wings I sing for joy. My soul sings to Thee; thy right hand upholds me (Psa. 63:6-8).

We can meditate upon the characteristics of God, such as His love, power, wisdom, grace, mercy, kindness, and patience. Psalm 77:12-15 teaches us to meditate upon the works of God:

> I will meditate on all Thy work, and muse on Thy deeds. Thy way, O God, is holy; what god is great like our God? Thou art the God who workest wonders; thou hast made known Thy strength among the peoples. Thou hast by Thy power redeemed Thy people, The sons of Jacob and Joseph.

There are many passages of Scripture that should cause us to meditate on the providence of God such as Psalm 107. As Christians, we can certainly meditate on God's redemption. God's promises are also legitimate objects of meditation. In Philippians, Paul urges Christians to reflect on those things that lead to Christian maturity:

Finally, brethren, whatever is true, whatever is honorable, whatever is right, whatever is pure, whatever is
lovely, whatever is of good repute, if there is any excellence and if anything worthy of praise, let your mind
dwell on these things (Phil. 4:8).

All these objects of meditation have one thing in common, they are all spoken of in the Word of God. Thus
meditation for the Christian should have for its primary
focus God's Word. Henri Nouwen comments:

We have, however, the words of Scripture to which to
pay attention. A psalm, a parable, a biblical story, a saying of Jesus, or a word of Paul, Peter, James, Jude, or
John can help us to focus our attention on God's presence . . . When we place words from the Scripture in the
center of solitude, such words – whether a short expression, a few sentences, or a larger text – can function as
the point to which we return when we have wandered
off in different directions.[67]

Most passages of Scripture dealing with meditation
have to do with meditation on the Word. Listen to the
Psalmist:

I will meditate on Thy precepts, and regard Thy ways. I
shall delight in Thy statutes; I shall not forget Thy word
(Psa. 119:15-16).

How do you go about meditating on the Word? Irving Jensen lists five very practical suggestions.[68]

1. REFLECT PURPOSEFULLY – Determine why you are
going to meditate on a specific passage. Is it to know
God more intimately? Is it to find God's will? Is it to

solve a problem? Meditate purposefully.

2. REFLECT IMAGINATIVELY – Meditation requires that you put yourself into the passage. Use your senses. Hear, see, taste, smell, and feel. This is easiest to do when the passage is a narrative. Be there. Experience it. If the passage is an exhortation, make yourself the recipient. A major element of meaningful meditation is a sanctified imagination.

3. REFLECT HUMBLY – Always remember that this is the very Word of God. "It should humble you to think that the Holy One, who is also the Almighty One, has spoken to you in the Bible and has given you the blessed privilege to read it, and through it to listen to Him."

4. REFLECT PRAYERFULLY – Meditation should lead to prayer and prayer to meditation. Thank God for the privilege of reflecting on His Word. Ask for His guidance in your reflections. Praise Him for His truth.

5. REFLECT PATIENTLY – Meditation requires not only solitude but time as well. The idea of "waiting on the Lord" is an essential element in meaningful meditation.

The whole point is that the Word of God becomes meaningful and applicable for our lives. There are many ways to appropriate the Word: hearing it preached and taught, reading it, studying it, and memorizing it. Personally, I carry a set of tapes in my car so I can listen to it. But the process of meditation may be the most thorough and personal way of appropriating the Word which is available to us. I'm told that to meditate means to ruminate. And one definition of ruminate is what a cow does when she chews her cud. It's not a particularly pleasant thought, but a cow eats, regurgitates the food out of the first of her four stomachs, and chews her food all over again. The food eventually goes into stomach two, three, and four, and then it finally is absorbed into the cow's blood stream.

I heard Bill Gothard tell how one year he meditated on Romans 6 for the entire twelve months. He read it, he studied it, he memorized it, but he also meditated on what it really means to be dead to sin. He made every principle and every word a part of his life.

Jim Downing writes, "As we meditate on the Word of God, the life of Jesus Christ flows out of Him, through the Word, and becomes a part of our spiritual bloodstream."[69] That's what meditation is really all about.

In surveying area preachers, I found a variety of meditation techniques being used. Several mentioned meditating while jogging. Others mentioned inspirational music as a springboard to meditation. Others emphasized going on walks with God. Kenneth Leech in his book *Soul Friend* recommends "slow reading of scripture, and 'brooding on the Word.' "[70]

I especially appreciated a practice by Dawson Trotman, founder of the Navigators. At night when he was ready to go to sleep he would say, "All right, H.W.L.W.," after which a passage of Scripture would be quoted without comment as the last word spoken. H.W.L.W. stood for His Word the Last Word. He was unknowingly practicing what psychologists would later discover, that the last dominant thought will stay in the subconscious during sleep.[71] "When I remember Thee

on my bed, I meditate on Thee in the night watches"
(Psa. 63:6).

REACT

As with the other disciplines, it is important to remember that neither solitude nor meditation are intended to be ends in themselves. It is how we react – what we do about the insights gained that really matters. Foster points out that "meditation is the one thing that can sufficiently redirect our lives so that we can deal with human life successfully."[72] Christ is honored and glorified through meditation only when it produces a reaction in our lives by which we accomplish God's will.

We are not called to a monastic life nor a life of contemplation alone. We are called to be light and salt in the world, to seek the lost and to glorify God by our good works.

William Barclay made this observation: "The more one reads of the lives and works of great men, the more one sees that they have a twin capacity – the capacity to work and the capacity to wait."[73] Jesus was the perfect example in that regard. He had just the right balance between doing and resting, speaking and listening, giving out and taking in.

Dr. E. Stanley Jones was for fifty years a missionary to India. He was a man who sought for this balance of which I speak. He wrote, "I found myself going off in solitude and reading my New Testament, and when I came across a verse that spoke of Him, I found myself reverently pressing my lips to that verse . . . But I'm soon up on my feet again with a compulsion, a divine compulsion to share this with everyone, everywhere."[74] That is the reaction of which I speak.

CONCLUSION

But right now I'm primarily concerned about your response to this chapter. Your response will be the most difficult for you to objectively evaluate. However, what you choose to do in response will very likely have a profound effect on all the other disciplines of which we have spoken and will speak.

Where does it all begin – the pursuit of solitude and the practice of meditation? I believe it starts with a desire for intimacy with God, the sort of intimacy known by man before the fall, the sort of walk with the Lord suggested by the old hymn:

IN THE GARDEN

I come to the garden alone, while the dew is still on the roses; and the voice I hear, falling on my ear, the Son of God discloses.

And He walks with me, and He talks with me, and He tells me I am His own, and the joy we share as we tarry there, none other has ever known.

He speaks, and the sound of His voice is so sweet the birds hush their singing; and the melody that He gave to me within my heart is ringing.

I'd stay in the garden with Him tho' the night around me be falling; but He bids me go thru the voice of woe,

His voice to me is calling.
  And He walks with me, and He talks with me, and He tells me I am His own, and the joy we share as we tarry there, none other has ever known.

THOUGHT QUESTIONS:

1. What did you think when you began reading this chapter on meditation? Did it make you uneasy?

2. Do you enjoy solitude? Why do you think so many people are threatened by the quiet?

3. How does solitude differ from loneliness?

4. How could you reorder your life so as to experience times of solitude?

5. The Psalmist delighted in meditating on the law of the Lord (Psa. 1:1-2). What things delight you and why?

6. What do you believe to be the primary benefit of meditation?

7. What do you think Paul meant when he wrote in Col. 3:2, "Set your mind on the things above . . . ?"

8. How will you try to incorporate the discipline of meditation into your devotional life?

SCRIPTURE REFERENCES:

Psa. 46:10	Josh. 1:8	Psa. 63:6-8
Matt. 14:13	Psa. 19:14	Psa. 77:12-15
Mark 6:31	Psa. 1:1-2	Phil. 4:8
Eph. 5:15-17	Col. 3:1-2	Psa. 119:15-16
Matt. 6:6		

RECOMMENDED READING:

Between Walden & The Whirlwind by Jean Fleming
Making All Things New by Henri Nouwen
Meditation by Jerry Downing
Meditation by Thomas McCormick & Sharon Fish

ASSIGNMENTS:

Read John 11:1-44 – As you read it, what stood out; what did you HEAR? Why do you think that word caught your attention?

Read John 11:1-44 again – What VISION stood out as you read? Is there any special significance for you personally in what you saw?

Read John 11:1-44 one more time – What FEELING did you have? Why do you think you identified that particular feeling?

What did the Lord say to you through this passage about your life and your service to Him?

In Psalm 119 there are eight different objects of meditation mentioned. Can you find them?

PRAYER:

"I pause, Father, to commence with you. Help me to be still and know that you are God. Ease awhile any tense muscles or strained nerves or wrought-up emotions. Let me be relaxed in body and calm in spirit so

that I may be more responsive to your presence. I pause,
Father, to commence with You . . . Amen."
                              –Roy E. Dickinson in Daily Prayer Companion

QUOTABLE QUOTES:

"The good is often the enemy of the best."
                                                            –unknown

"It is God who wishes to establish communication. He is
more anxious to speak to us than we are to hear Him.
He is incredibly persistent in trying to get through. Our
real problem is that we tend to avoid hearing Him."
                              –From THE FIGHT by John White

"Our practical, materialistic society so values action
over meditation, study, and prayer that we often feel
guilty when we stop to think, study, or pray."
–From BETWEEN WALDEN & THE WHIRLWIND by
                                                      Jean Fleming

"Meditating is that 'remembering' so vital to praise."
                              –Edmund P. Clowney

"Earth's crammed with heaven and every common bush
aflame with God; but only those who see take off their
shoes, the rest sit around it and pluck blackberries."
                              –Elizabeth Barrett Browning

Chapter Seven

GROWING THROUGH THE DEVOTIONAL LIFE

In the morning, O Lord, Thou wilt hear my voice; In the morning I will order my prayer to Thee and eagerly watch (Psa. 5:3).

"The Morning Watch" is just one of many designations for a personal quiet time, or devotions. It was a term that came from the campus of Cambridge University in 1882. Students were weighed down with studies, lectures, athletics, and the other distractions of college life. Christian students, including two by the name of Hooper and Thornton, knew that they were floundering spiritually. They sought an answer and came up with the morning watch – a plan to spend the first minutes of each day alone with God, praying and reading His

Word. They realized that to know God requires consistently spending time with Him.

The idea caught on and a time of religious revival followed at Cambridge and resulted in the departure of the Cambridge Seven, a group of prominent athletes and men of wealth and education, for missionary service in China.

Calvin Coolidge once remarked, "People criticize me for harping on the obvious. Yet if all the folks in the United States would do the few simple things they know they ought to do, most of our big problems would take care of themselves."[75] What he said is true of a Christian's devotional life. Call it whatever you will – the morning watch, the quiet time, devotions, or personal worship – a special time set aside each day for prayer, Bible study, meditation, and communion with God is essential to spiritual vitality and intimacy with Christ. Robert Foster says:

> It's the golden thread that ties every great man of God together – from Moses to David Livingstone, the prophet Amos to Billy Graham – rich and poor, businessmen and military personnel. Every man who ever became somebody for God has this at the core of his priorities: time alone with God![76]

Foster is right. If proof is needed for the importance of the devotional life, the writings and lives of great men of God through the ages provide it. However, the best proof of all is found in the example of Jesus who, "In the early morning, while it was still dark, He arose and went out and departed to a lonely place, and was praying there" (Mark 1:35).

In the past several chapters we have been dealing with such specific Christian disciplines as prayer, Bible study, confession, journaling, and meditation. All are important ingredients in the devotional life. But today it is time to start integrating these elements into a specific daily devotional time or quiet time. When first surveyed, only 36% of our people had a consistent, daily, devotional time. Nearly two-thirds did not. It has been my intent from the beginning to encourage you to begin or to improve your own personal, devotional life. Not only is that tremendously important to your own spiritual vitality; but it is absolutely essential to the revitalization of the church.

I am under no illusions about this coming about easily. For most of us it requires a restructuring of our schedules, even getting up earlier in the morning which for some is a horrendous task. Of the college boys at Cambridge who were determined to have their "morning watch" Thornton had the most difficulty in this matter of getting out of bed. However, he put together a contraption by his bed by which the vibration of his alarm clock set some fishing tackle in motion and the covers, fastened to the line, were quickly pulled off his sleeping body. Hopefully few of us would have to go to such drastic measures, but it does take effort. It does take discipline. One preacher who was over 55 years of age wrote in response to my survey, "I have found this the most difficult discipline of my whole life."

Several years ago, Arnold Palmer was being interviewed while he was practicing on the putting green. "Arnie," he was asked, "what do you feel was wrong to make you play so poorly this past year?" Without looking up from his putter, he answered, "I wasn't hard enough on myself, that's all." Two hours later the interviewer passed by the putting green and noticed that the legendary golfer was still practicing. The reporter observed, "The greatness of Arnold Palmer is his choice of the hard way."[77]

Palmer was illustrating what Jesus was teaching in a much more serious area than golf when He said in Matthew 7:13-14:

> Enter by the narrow gate; for the gate is wide, and the way is broad that leads to destruction, and many are those who enter by it. For the gate is small, and the way is narrow that leads to life, and few are those who find it.

Dr. Maxie Dunnam, in commenting on the life of discipline, writes:

> Discipline is an absolute necessity for the Christian life. We may be converted to Christ in the miracle of a moment, but becoming a saint is the task of a lifetime . . . As Christians we do not emerge full-blown; we grow. We grow by discipline. So let's be clear as we begin. Discipline is not an end in itself. In the history of Christianity, that thought has not always prevailed and disciplines themselves have become THE THING. We have made discipline an end, not a means. We have even used it as a proof of our 'sainthood.' That is the reason Christianity is often presented as a somber, self-denying, world-denying way that produces pinch-faced sadness. Jesus presented something else. He called us to the joy of a wedding banquet, to the dance of celebration over a lost son who has come home. But we experience that freedom of joy and celebration only as we are

willing to see the kingdom as a pearl of great price for which we are willing to exchange all else.[78]

Do you see the kingdom in that light? Does Christ mean more to you than anyone or anything else? Do you long for the most intimate possible walk with your Lord? Are you willing to pay the price of discipline? Then the devotional life is for you. Let's look at its development in the Preliminaries, the Procedure, and the Profit.

THE PRELIMINARIES

If we only did what we wanted to do and only when we wanted to do it, our lives would be in utter chaos. Many Christians' lives are in utter spiritual chaos. Most Christians do not have a consistent, daily devotional life, not because they don't think it is important, but because they do not make it a priority, they don't discipline themselves in this area of life. To develop a successful devotional life the Christian must PRIORITIZE TIME WITH GOD.

You take time to eat. You take time to sleep. The reason is because you know these things are essential to physical life and health. Without sleep, you would soon be unable to function. Without food, hunger pangs would soon remind you of your need. Let me urge you to develop an awareness of your need to spend time with God. The Psalmist wrote, "As the deer pants for the water brooks, so my soul pants for Thee, O God. My soul thirsts for God, for the living God; when shall I come and appear before God?" (Psa. 41:1-2). In verse 7 of the same chapter, he writes, "Deep calls to deep." You and I need to be aware of a call to deeper, fuller living. Don't be content with a passing acquaintance with Christ. Don't be satisfied with shallow teaching and superficial experiences. There is a need, a longing, a hunger deep within you for closer communion with God. Make the devotional life a priority.

The next preliminary is to HAVE THE RIGHT TIME AND PLACE. For most of us it is in the early morning. For a few it will be late at night. The only real alternatives for most of us would be during the lunch hour or right after work or school. The important thing is consistency. The same is true of the place. Although it is best to find a quiet and private place, it is probably even more important that you consistently use the same place. Most of us function far better with routine or ritual in our lives. As to the amount of time, again regularity and consistency are even more important than quality. Ten minutes each day is far more valuable than two hours once a week. However, most of us can surely set aside more time than that. Plan to grow in your devotional life and thus in the time spent.

A third preliminary is GO TO BED. Here is one of my problems. I'll start watching TV or get really involved in a book and I don't want to go to bed. The only problem is, I'm not rested, refreshed, and ready for my quiet time the next morning. We're talking about disciplines. Ball players have a curfew so that they can compete well in an athletic event. Surely we as Christians should be just as disciplined for the game of life.

The next preliminary is GET UP. Believe me, when you start setting that alarm clock earlier so that you can have time with God, you'll find all sorts of excuses for why you should stay in bed just a little longer.

When you get up, make sure you WAKE UP. You might think that I'm confused and that I have that backwards. You may think you should wake up and then get up. No, I'm speaking from experience. Some people have their quiet time immediately after getting out of bed. I've tried that and it doesn't work for me because I'm not yet alert. I have a routine. I get up a little after six and I work out, I exercise. Then I shower, shave and get dressed for the day. I go out and get the newspaper and read it while I eat breakfast. THEN I go to my quiet place for my quiet time where I stay until I go to the office at eight o'clock. Now I pray before I ever get out of bed. And I often meditate while I'm riding my exercise bike. But I want to be fully awake and alert when I enter into my special quiet time with God.

The next preliminary is to ASSEMBLE YOUR DEVOTIONAL HELPS. For me that means gathering my Bible, my devotional guide, my prayer diary, my journal, and whatever book I happen to be reading.

Another very important preliminary is that you EXPECT GOD'S PRESENCE. In the little book *Quiet Time* from InterVarsity we read:

> Expectancy is another necessity. He who expects nothing will get nothing. It is the eager soul that will be made glad. If we will expose all our soul to the Holy Spirit, we shall have many a thrilling surprise . . . Be quiet. Concentrate. Expect.[79]

Finally, HAVE AN OBJECTIVE. Actually there should be two primary objectives to your devotional life. First is for spiritual growth and nourishment. The Word is food for spiritual growth. It is spoken of as milk, honey, bread, and meat. However, the objective of the devotional life is not just for growth and nourishment but for personal, vital fellowship with the Lord Jesus Christ. Paul tells us in I Corinthians 1:9 that "God is faithful, through whom you were called into fellowship with His Son, Jesus Christ our Lord." It is in the devotional life that that fellowship is cultivated and deepened. What a life-changing experience that can be. David wrote of such a life, "Thou wilt make known to me the path of life; In Thy presence is fullness of joy; In Thy right hand there are pleasures forever" (Psa. 16:11).

Before we go further, let's review the preliminaries. Prioritize your devotional life. Have the right time and place. Go to bed. Get up. Wake up. Assemble your devotional helps. Expect God's presence. And have an objective. Now we're ready to proceed.

THE PROCEDURE

Let me begin by making it clear that there is no one proper procedure. It is not important that your quiet time be like mine or that mine be like yours. Over the years, I've used many different procedures. I've read the Bible through in a year and prayed over the ideas brought to mind by each day's reading. I've used the devotional guide, *Prayer Time: A Guide For Personal Wor-*

ship by Don DeWelt published by College Press. DeWelt divides each devotional time into twelve periods and his book is very thorough and helpful. I've included a chart of the twelve periods at the end of the chapter. For the last two years I've used *A Guide To Prayer For Ministers And Other Servants* by Reuben Job and Norman Shawchuck and published by The Upper Room. Because it is especially geared to vocational Christian workers, it has been a very special blessing in my life.

This year I am using *Disciplines For The Inner Life* by Bob and Michael W. Benson as my devotional guide. It, too, is excellent. Please keep in mind that I am in no way suggesting that you need to follow this particular model. But let me just walk you through my own personal practice which is simply an expansion of Benson's book.

I begin with a prayer invoking God's blessing on my quiet time and asking special guidance for whatever the theme of the day may be. Next, I read the Psalm suggested by the guide. Actually I read the same Psalm every day for seven days. Each day new ideas, insights, and truths seem to jump right off the page. By the way, I find it to be much more meaningful and easier to concentrate when I read the Scriptures out loud.

I also read a chapter from Proverbs each day. I read the chapter corresponding to the day of the month. As there are 31 chapters in Proverbs, I read this tremendous collection of God-inspired wisdom 12 times each year.

Benson's guide also suggests another Scripture reading for each day of the week, most often from the New Testament. This is in keeping with the theme of the day and the week. As we read devotionally, it is important that we keep asking the questions we learned to ask in the message on Bible study: What does it say? What does it mean? How does it apply to my life?

It is also important to approach devotional Bible reading with a certain attitude. A.J. Conyers writes:

> That which makes Bible reading a devotional reading is more than a method, it is an attitude – even a certain passion – a willingness to go outside of ourselves in the discovery of that which is greater and infinitely more important than we are. It is a realization that we are confronted by a superior Word that renders all our lesser words as chaff driven before the wind. There is all the difference in the world between an approach to the text in which we sit as the judge, applying our critical faculties in study, and an approach which puts us figuratively or literally on our knees, willing to have our own lives judged by the searchlight of God's Word.[80]

Following the reading of God's Word comes the reading of a passage from some great devotional classic, ancient or contemporary. On the day I was preparing this chapter the selection was by Glaphre Gilliland. It dealt with how we seek our own goals and then ask God's approval and blessing, how we depend on our own wisdom when God's wisdom is available to us. I must tell you that it really struck home with me. It made a difference. It blessed my life.

A time of meditation on the Word and on the devotional selection is next. Now I may stop to meditate as I read. However, I take some time just to be quiet, be open, reflect, and listen to God. That leads into a very natural time to write in my journal. To be honest, once I start writing I want to keep on and journaling could consume the time I need to spend in prayer. But as we've already learned, keeping a journal can be a very significant part of the process of spiritual growth in our lives.

The next major part of my quiet time is devoted to prayer. There is nothing more important. Christian history demonstrates time and time again that those men and women who have moved this world for God have been people who have been well disciplined in prayer. Martin Luther said, "If I fail to spend two hours in prayer each morning, the devil gets the victory through the day. I have so much business I cannot get on without three hours daily in prayer." Adoniram Judson suggested, "Arrange thy affairs, if possible so that thou canst leisurely devote two or three hours every day not merely to devotional exercises but to the very act of secret prayer and communion with God."[81] I know of no one today who even approaches such a mark. But I recall these as I could dozens of others from history to simply underscore prayer's priority. These men prayed three hours and yet the average Christian of today prays three minutes. May we be convicted of the urgency and primacy of prayer.

Personally I try to follow the acrostic A-C-T-S (Adoration, Confession, Thanksgiving, and Supplication). I spend time in adoring or praising the Lord for who He is and what He has done. I spend time in confession of my known sins and in asking Him to make known to me those sins of which I am not aware. Next I spend time in thanksgiving, an inexhaustible subject. But most of my prayer time is devoted to supplication or petition. Here I work from four separate prayer lists.

First, I pray for those matters on my list of immediate needs. This includes the physically ill, the bereaved, and matters of urgency which have been brought to my attention. Next I pray for all those matters on my ongoing list. This includes family members, long-term goals, and personal struggles. Next I pray for my "Ten Most Wanted List." I identify ten persons I want to see won to Christ and I pray for them daily and work at building relationships and having opportunities to witness to them. One of the great joys of my life is that of taking people off that list that we've seen come to Christ, and replacing them with someone else who needs the Lord. Finally, I have a list that is divided according to the days of the week. Here I pray for missionaries, colleges and seminaries, parachurch organizations, friends, churches and various other projects that are dear to my heart. From time to time I also pray through our entire church membership list, praying for each member by name and by need if I am aware of that need. I also find reading and praying the prayers of others to be a very helpful practice that continually deepens and broadens my own personal prayer life.

After my prayer time, the devotional guide suggests a hymn. Again, the hymn is to be read or sung each day for seven days. Again and again I've been blessed by the tremendous message in hymns – hymns I've sung again and again and yet never really taken the time to appreciate.

Finally I read a benediction from the devotional

guide and then I usually read a chapter from whatever Christian book I happen to be working on. The whole process I've just described could be carried out in as little as fifteen or twenty minutes. Thirty to forty minutes is more adequate. However, it is a tremendous thing to have no time constraints and to be able to spend an hour or even more in this quiet time with the Lord.

Again, it is important that you not think the model I've described to be "the" only model or even the right model for you. It works for me. It incorporates and integrates most of the spiritual disciplines we've been talking about. But if you have another method that meets your needs, use it. But do use something. Perhaps you'll develop your own procedure just using the Bible. That's great! But most of us really need a devotional guide of some sort. Perhaps the best known of all devotional guides is *My Utmost For His Highest* by Oswald Chambers. It is a devotional classic around which you could build the other disciplines. An even simpler approach to get you started might be the use of a devotional magazine such as *Our Daily Bread* or *The Upper Room* or *Devotion*. I've listed the addresses for these and other devotional magazines at the end of the chapter.

The resources are there. The importance is unquestioned. A consistent, daily devotional life is essential to spiritual vitality, growth, and health. Will you do it? Will you make the commitment to get started this week? Remember, the most nutritious of food is of no benefit to a starving man if he refuses to eat. But when a starving man partakes of that food, it means the difference between life and death.

PROFIT

Over the years, I've struggled and struggled in the area of the devotional life. More often than not, I've only felt guilty because I knew I wasn't really doing what I should have been doing. Although I've always been a hard worker and would appear to most people to be a disciplined person, this is an area of my life in which discipline has not come easily. However, as the church has grown and my responsibilities have increased – as I've been thrust into the arena of helping people with increasingly complex problems – as Satan's personal attacks on me and on the church at Kingsway have increased – I've realized that this was an area of my life where changes had to take place.

I haven't arrived. I'm not attempting to set myself up as some sort of example. But I know how far I've come and I know I wouldn't still be at Kingsway and perhaps I wouldn't be in the ministry at all if it were not for what I've learned about the importance and the practice of the devotional life. What I've found to be true has been the experience of many others. I talked with another pastor whose church has been under continuous assault and he shared how it was only his devotional life that had enabled him to hang in there. He said, "This (his devotional life) has been my greatest area of growth and joy in my life these last two years." He's spending over an hour a day in prayer, keeping a spiritual journal, fasts regularly, has made himself spiritually accountable to certain others, is faithfully into the Word for personal spiritual growth, and read twenty-seven books last year for that purpose.

Another area preacher wrote:

> A personal daily prayer and devotional life was the tool that probably saved me as a minister. A few years ago I went through a terrible spiritual attack of burnout and depression. The load I was carrying crippled me and I discovered my inner, personal resources spiritually were almost nil. I entered into a discipline of walking 3 miles every morning followed by an hour of scripture reading and prayer. The recovery effects were amazing to me and I believe the overall effect was God leading me into (a new ministry) which has challenged the disciplines I had set up.

Don't you see, the devotional life is not just desirable, it is essential to spiritual survival if we are going to be out there battling on the front lines for our Lord. We can never overemphasize the teaching of Ephesians 6:12-13:

> For our struggle is not against flesh and blood, but against the rulers, against the powers, against the world forces of this darkness, against the spiritual forces of wickedness in the heavenly places. Therefore, take up the full armor of God, that you may be able to resist in the evil day, and having done everything to stand firm.

However, I do not want to leave in your minds mere survival as the primary profit of the devotional life, for the greatest benefit is simply that of knowing Christ more fully, more personally, more passionately. Again the little book, *Quiet Time*, speaks to my heart in this regard:

> There is a passion for Christ which it has been given to very few to possess, but which has set those who have it

apart for ever from their fellow men. Is not this the quality which separates between Christian and Christian, which marks out some – the rare ones – as being apart from the rest of us? Is it not this quality in the writing of the mystics which, as in no other spiritual literature, pulls at our heart strings and creates a pain of longing?

Those marvelous "friends of God" had the personal passion for Christ. Samuel Rutherford had it too, and in his bleak prison he could write, "One smile of Christ's face is now to me as a kingdom. The trouble with the rest of us is that we are content to dwell in Jerusalem without seeing the face of the King. We are hard at work for him; the freighted hours rush by leaving us scarcely time to give a thought to the Lover of our souls who is longing for our friendship. And when we do go into the audience chamber, we are burdened with requests – business that must be put through, guidance we need here, help there, petitions on behalf of this one or that. All important, all urgent, all worthy, but – just business. Amidst the terrific onrush of the apostasy, amidst the swirl of pleasure which is engulfing the majority of those who call themselves Christians, God has his own, his seven thousand, "all the knees which have not bowed to Baal, and every mouth which has not kissed him."

They are men and women whose faith and zeal burn brighter as the world's darkness deepens. They are ready to die at Jerusalem, or anywhere, for their Lord. They are valiant for the truth, and wield the sword lustily on God's behalf. Nevertheless, few have that passion for Christ which Paul expressed in the words, 'To me to live is Christ.'

There is so much splendid orthodoxy that leaves people cold, so much preaching of "the simple gospel" that excites no enthusiasm. People can sit and listen to the story of Calvary with dry eyes and no quickened heartbeat. IN THE TELLING OF THAT STORY THERE IS NO RING OF PERSONAL PASSION FOR THE ONE FROM WHOSE 'HEAD, AND HANDS, AND FEET, SORROW AND LOVE FLOW MINGLED DOWN.' But now and again – at rare intervals – one meets someone who, like Paul, has looked into the matchless face of Jesus, and who henceforth sees nothing save the face of his Beloved.

Paul might easily have become hard and critical and bitter in the stress of controversial conflict. The passion for the person of Christ, as apart from loyalty to his cause, kept him from that. And so, speaking after the manner of men, we see him fighting the beasts of Ephesus, and yet homesick to "depart and be with Christ, which is far better." The great tender heart of love in Paul that made him the nursing father of the infant churches had its fountainhead in his all-absorbing personal passion for Christ, to know the love of whom – its breadth, and length, and depth and height – is to be "filled with all the fullness of God."

There is reward for the obedient disciples, there is power and authority for the faithful disciples, there is glory of achievement for the zealous disciple . . . but there is the whisper of God's love, there is the joy of his presence, and the shining of his face for those who love him for himself alone. And "to what profit is it that we dwell in Jerusalem, if we do not see the face of the King?"[82]

CONCLUSION

May you desire such a passion for Christ that you will seek it and find it in your own personal, consistent, daily, devotional time with our Lord.

I need Thee every hour, most gracious Lord;
No tender voice like Thine can peace afford.
I need Thee; O, I need Thee; every hour I need Thee!
O bless me now, my Saviour, I come to thee.
I need Thee every hour, stay Thou near by;
Temptations lose their power when Thou art nigh.

I need Thee every hour in joy or pain;
Come quickly and abide, or life is vain.
  I need Thee every hour, most Holy One;
O make me Thine indeed, Thou blessed Son.
  I need Thee; O, I need Thee; every hour I need Thee!
O bless me now, my Saviour, I come to thee.

THOUGHT QUESTIONS

1. What has been the primary barrier to your personal development of (or improvement of) your devotional life?

2. Do you consider it important? Why or why not?

3. In the past, many Christians have spent hours in Bible study, meditation and prayer. Why do you believe that is virtually unheard of in the America of today?

4. If you were to set aside a time for devotions, when would it be? Will you do it?

5. What do you believe would be the major changes in your congregation if everyone were to be seriously involved in a consistent, daily, devotional time?

6. What images does the word "discipline" bring to mind? Why is discipline so important in the devotional life?

7. What procedures do you use (would you use) in your quiet time?

8. What do you consider the greatest benefit of a vibrant devotional life?

9. Can you identify with the reading on "A Passion for Christ"? If "no," why not? If "yes," in what ways?

10. How would you evaluate your personal spiritual growth? What relationship do you see between your answer and your practice of the devotional life?

ASSIGNMENTS:

Stop by a Christian bookstore this week and look over their selection of devotional guides.

Make a covenant with God to set aside a time each day to spend time alone with Him; but beware of making a commitment which goes beyond your ability to carry through. (Remember, consistency and regularity are more important initially than quantity.)

Read the following verses and then summarize what they say about the importance of the Word of God to spiritual growth and nourishment: I Peter 2:2; Psalm 119:103; Jeremiah 15:16; Hebrews 5:12-14.

Read the following verses and then summarize what they teach about the importance of a close, personal walk with the Lord: I Cor. 1:9; John 15:4; Micah 6:8; Psalm 16:11; Psalm 23.

SCRIPTURE REFERENCES:

Psalm 5:3	I Cor. 1:9
Mark 1:35	Psalm 16:11
Matt. 7:13-14	Eph. 6:12-13
Psalm 42:1-2, 7	

RECOMMENDED READING:

My Utmost For His Highest by Oswald Chambers
Quiet Time: A Practical Guide For Daily Devotions from InterVarsity
This Morning With God edited by Carol Adeney
Growing Deep In The Christian Life by Charles Swindoll

DEVOTIONAL MAGAZINES:

Daily Meditation – Box 2710, San Antonio, TX 78299
The Daily Walk – P.O. Box 80587, Atlanta, GA 30366
Devotion – 8121 Hamilton Ave., Cincinnati, OH 45231
Our Daily Bread – P.O. Box 22, Grand Rapids, MI 49555
Pathway To God – P.O. Box 2499, Anderson, IN 46011
Power For Today – 2809 Granny White Pike, Nashville, TN 37204
The Upper Room – 1908 Grand Avenue, Nashville, TN 37202

DEVOTIONAL MODEL: (From PRAYER TIME by Don DeWelt)

QUOTABLE QUOTES:

"The men who have most fully illustrated Christ in their character, and have most powerfully affected the world for Him, have been men who spend so much time with God as to make it a notable feature in their lives . . . To be little with God is to be little for God."

–E.M. Bounds

"That God desires our fellowship is, perhaps, one of the most amazing facts conveyed to us through the Scriptures."

–from *Quiet Time*

"Make perfectly clear to yourself each day as you begin your Quiet Time that you cannot convey to others divine grace if you yourself have a neglected spiritual condition."

–from *Quiet Time*

Chapter Eight

GROWING THROUGH FASTING

And whenever you fast, do not put on a gloomy face as the hypocrites do; for they neglect their appearance in order to be seen fasting by men. Truly I say to you, they have their reward in full. But you, when you fast, anoint your head, and wash your face; so that you may not be seen fasting by men, but by your Father who is in secret; and your Father who sees in secret will repay you (Matt. 6:16-18).

My favorite cartoon is Calvin and Hobbes. That six year old brat, Calvin, and his stuffed tiger, Hobbes, who comes to life in Calvin's imaginary world, really get into some interesting situations. Recently Calvin was feigning sickness for his babysitter, who knowing Calvin's tricks, pretended to call the doctor and then announced the prescribed treatment. Calvin was to be given a dose of castor oil and put to bed. In the last frame Calvin, looking puzzled, asks, "What's castor oil?"

My experiences with castor oil were quite different. I knew all too well what it was. And although I was basically an obedient child, when the castor oil bottle came out, I took off, no matter how sick I was. I far preferred a switching with the wild cherry tree limb to a dose of that awful stuff.

The two basic responses of Christians to the subject of fasting parallel those of Calvin and me to castor oil. Most Christians are woefully ignorant on the whole subject. Others know something about it but consider it the most distasteful of the Christian disciplines. Well, the fact is that fasting is not nearly as distasteful as some people make it out to be; and ignorance on the subject is certainly wrong, for Jesus made it clear that He expected us to fast. He didn't say, "If you fast," but, "WHENEVER you fast."

No, fasting is not an entrance requirement for heaven nor can I show you the first verse commanding that you fast. However, I do hope to show you the Biblical importance of fasting and the practical benefits to the extent that some of you who have never fasted will be challenged and motivated to enter into a new spiritual discipline that may very well help you win some victories that would otherwise not be won.

Most people have never fasted. That is not surprising in a society that places little emphasis on self-denial and in an age where the church has almost completely ignored the subject. Specifically, the Spiritual Disciplines Survey showed that 53.3 percent of our members had never fasted, not even once. Only 1 percent said they fast regularly. Among area ministers, 9 percent had never fasted and only 8 percent fasted on a regular basis while 59 percent say they have fasted several times. Obviously we are dealing with a discipline that has not been over-emphasized.

While it is not my intention to attempt an exhaustive treatment of the subject, we will look at the past of fasting, the purpose of fasting, and the practice of fasting. To put it another way, we will survey the history of fasting both Biblically and in the church through the centuries; we'll look at why we should fast, and finally at how we should go about it.

THE PAST OF FASTING

How many references to fasting do you suppose are in the Bible? Most of you will be surprised to know that there are at least 123 such references. In Don DeWelt's extensive treatise called *Prayer and Fasting,* he comments on each one.[83] We won't take the time for that but it is significant that there are so many references.

Moses neither ate nor drank for 40 days on the mountain. Hannah fasted when she wanted a son from God. King David fasted on several occasions recorded in Scripture. Elijah fasted forty days after his juniper tree experience. The whole nation of Israel fasted. Through fasting and prayer Nehemiah gained permission to return to Jerusalem. Esther had the Jews fast three days and nights. In Daniel nine, Daniel fasted three weeks as he sought an answer to prayer.

But what about fasting in the New Testament? The prophetess Anna served the Lord in the temple with fastings and prayer at the time of the birth of Jesus (Luke 2:37). John the Baptist fasted. Matthew four describes Jesus' fast of forty days (Matt. 4:2). In the Sermon on the Mount Jesus assumed that His disciples would fast. After Paul (then known as Saul) saw the Lord on the road to Damascus, he fasted for three days in a fast of repentance. Paul said he fasted often. Fasting preceded the commissioning of Paul and Barnabas as missionaries in Acts thirteen. It is obvious that fasting was a Biblical practice.

Throughout the history of the church, there have been many notable men of God who sought God's power and blessing while fasting. If you choose to fast, you are in the company of such people as Martin Luther, John Calvin, John Knox, Jonathan Edwards, David Brainerd, R.A. Torrey, Andrew Murray, John Wesley, and Charles Finney. The ancient church is filled with testimonies to the importance of fasting.

However, something happened along the line. Richard Foster in researching the subject of fasting found not one book published on the subject from 1861 to 1954, a period of nearly one hundred years. Although there is a renewed interest in fasting today, my search of the libraries turned up only about a dozen volumes on the subject today from a spiritual perspective. Perhaps this lack of emphasis is due to the excesses of asceticism and self-mortification sometimes practiced by certain segments of the church in the past. Or perhaps it is a reflection of the self-serving lifestyle of modern day man which avoids self-denial of any sort. Whatever the reasons, the modern day lack of emphasis is in contradiction to the past history of fasting both in Biblical days and in the church through the centuries.

What was the nature of these fasts? Actually there were and are three types of fasts. A normal fast is one in which a person eats no food but continues to take in liquids. Such was the case when Jesus fasted forty days and nights. The Bible tells us that He became hungry but does not mention thirst, for most Biblical scholars believe Jesus drank water in the wilderness even while eating no food. However, on occasion there were complete fasts. In Acts 9:9 concerning the conversion of Saul of Tarsus, it says he "neither ate nor drank." When Ezra was in mourning over the unfaithfulness of God's people, Ezra 10:6 tells us, "he did not eat bread, nor drink water." Then there were also partial fasts which involved abstaining from certain foods. Daniel mentions such a fast in Daniel 10:3 where he says, "I did not eat any tasty food, nor did meat or wine enter my mouth, nor did I use any ointment at all, until the entire three weeks were completed."

Arthur Wallis offers a modern day illustration of a partial fast in telling of a Russian believer who went to stay on the farm of a Christian couple in England several years ago. Having been converted to Christ she had worked for the Lord in a displaced persons camp in Austria. She declined all but the simplest of foods from her British hosts, saying that she could not do otherwise while her brothers and sisters among whom she had labored were enduring such hardship. Wallis comments, "God never fails to honor such self-denial."[84]

There are other Biblical examples of people whose partial fast was a way of life. Perhaps the best known is John the Baptist who lived on locusts and wild honey, a rather restricted and simple diet. A partial fast is also sometimes defined as skipping certain meals to devote oneself to prayer.

Brief as it may have been, I hope our survey of the history of fasting has established it in your mind as credible and important from both a Biblical and church history perspective. Arthur Wallis puts this historical perspective in poetic form:

> On Sinai's mount, with radiant face,
> To intercede for heaven's grace
> Upon a stubborn, wayward race,
> He fasted.
> Once lifted from the miry clay,
> When opposition came his way
> This soldier-king would often pray
> With fasting.
> A seer, possessed of vision keen,
> Who told the troubled king his dream,
> Had light on God's prophetic scheme
> Through fasting.
> The prophetess in temple court
> Beheld the Babe the two had brought;
> For Him she long had prayed and sought,
> With fasting.
> He came to break the yoke of sin,
> But ere His mission could begin
> He met the foe and conquered him
> With fasting.
> "Set these apart," the Spirit bade,

A spring, that soon vast rivers made,
Broke ope by men who as they prayed
Were fasting.
   When we shall stand on that great day
And give account, what shall we say,
If He should ask us, "Did you pray –
With fasting?"[85]

THE PURPOSE OF FASTING

Richard Foster defines fasting by saying:

The central idea in fasting is the voluntary denial of an otherwise normal function for the sake of intense spiritual activity.[86]

Given that definition, and given the fact that fasting is Biblical, the question still arises as to whether or not it is a command binding on Christians today. Jesus dealt with it in the same context as giving and praying. All are considered as acts of devotion to God which must come from a proper attitude and proper motivation. Jesus assumed His disciples would give, pray, and fast. He said, "When you give . . . when you pray . . . when you fast . . . " (Matt. 6:2,5,17). He did not say "If you give . . . if you pray . . . if you fast." However, it is true that there is no specific command telling the Christian to fast. Thus the purpose of fasting is not one of simple obedience.

Neither is the purpose of fasting that of proving yourself pious or impressing God. If there were any question about that, it should be answered by the reading of Colossians 2:20-23:

If you have died with Christ to the elementary principles of the world, why, as if you were living in the
world, do you submit yourself to decrees, such as, "Do
not handle, do not taste, do not touch!" (which all refer
to things destined to perish with the using) – in accor-
dance with the commandments and teachings of men?
These are matters which have, to be sure, the appearance of wisdom in self-made religion and self-abase-
ment and severe treatment of the body, but are of no
value against fleshly indulgence.

Paul makes the same point in Romans 14:17 where he
writes, "The Kingdom of God is not eating and drinking, but righteousness and peace and joy in the Holy
Spirit." Again he writes in I Corinthians 8:8, "But food
will not commend us to God; we are neither the worse if
we do not eat, nor the better if we do eat." You won't
impress God with what you do or don't eat. Nor will
fasting, in itself, make you a godly person anymore than
any other legalistic practice.

What then is the purpose of fasting if it has no particular spiritual merit in and of itself? When Jesus taught
fasting in the Sermon on the Mount His emphasis was
on the motivation behind it rather than the act itself.
The purpose was not to be recognition nor a bargaining
tool with God. Instead it was to be a matter of submis-
sion to the Lord, designed to honor Him. That has
always been its purpose and the motivation has always
been God's concern. He spoke to the people of Zechariah's day through the prophet in Zechariah 7:5:

Say to all the people of the land and to the priests,
"When you fasted and mourned in the fifth and seventh
months these seventy years, was it actually for Me that
you fasted?"

The primary purpose of fasting must be to please Him. Fasting should draw attention to God, not to the person fasting.

Fasting also brings more power to prayer. Have you noticed how many times fasting is mentioned in conjunction with prayer? When Jesus drove the demon from the demonized boy of Matthew 17, the disciples asked why they had been unable to do it. Jesus answered, "This kind does not go out except by prayer and fasting" (Matt. 17:21). There is special power in prayer accompanied by fasting. When Daniel faced spiritual hindrances, he fasted and prayed and God responded in a powerful way. When Ezra wanted to seek the Lord's protection for himself and his companions in their return to Palestine, he fasted and prayed and the Lord responded (Ezra 8:23). And who can forget how the people of Nineveh repented at the preaching of Jonah and how they fasted and prayed that God would spare their city and Jonah 3:10 tells us, "God relented concerning the calamity which He had declared He would bring upon them. And He did not do it." Prayer backed up by fasting changed the very mind of God.

Another benefit and purpose of fasting is that it helps to keep the body in its place. It is one way of proving that we are not to be numbered among those of whom Paul spoke in Philippians 3:19 when he said their "god is their appetite." Believe me, this is no small matter. Again and again the Scriptures teach us to make sure that our physical appetites are under control rather than in control. "Flee youthful lusts" (II Tim. 2:22)."Deny ungodliness and worldly desires" (Titus 2:12). "Abstain from fleshly lusts" (I Pet. 2:11). "Make no provision for the flesh in regard to its lusts" (Rom. 13:14). Paul further elaborates on the importance of self-discipline in I Corinthians 9:25-27:

> And everyone who competes in the games exercises self-control in all things. They then do it to receive a perishable wreath, but we an imperishable. Therefore I run in such a way, as not without aim; I box in such a way, as not beating the air; but I buffet my body and make it my slave, lest possibly, after I have preached to others, I myself should be disqualified.

Tildon Edwards comments on fasting as it relates to our physical appetites:

> Fasting also can simplify the compulsive, distracting, grasping nature of our appetites. When we fast intentionally, one of the first things we notice is how little food we really need, yet how much we have been wolfing down. The dull, bloated feeling from over-eating slowly vanishes. We become lighter and more lucid. We see that we really are capable of not responding to that grasping wave of appetite that clicks in our brain. That is a little realization of freedom. If we don't respond to that shallow, driving wave, we are free to flow in a simpler, deeper, more even-flowing stream.[87]

It should be at least mentioned that fasting serves several purely physical purposes as well, one being the physical cleansing of the body. However, that is not our primary concern today.

Fasting does help us think more clearly and it enhances spiritual perception. Physically, the head doesn't have to compete with the digestive system. In an extended fast your physical desires are dulled and your spiritual senses come alive. On various occasions, I have fasted for several days at a time and I know that by the third day, you are almost oblivious to any physical cravings, leaving you free to concentrate on things of the Spirit. Far more often I fast only for 36 hours and in such a fast the hunger itself is a reminder of the fast and thus a reminder to pray. Fasting, rightly observed, draws us toward God.

The Pharisees of Jesus' day had come to observe fasting as a ritual with intrinsic spiritual benefit. Jesus condemned them for their ritualistic practice which they tried to bind on other people but which was void of meaning. Again, fasting is intended by God to serve a specific purpose, to move toward an identifiable goal. Oswald Sanders identifies four such situations:

1) The challenge of a special test or temptation.
2) A deep yearning after a closer walk with God.
3) A heavy burden for the spread of the Gospel to the regions beyond.
4) The urgency of a difficult situation.[88]

The New Testament examples which we have, all have to do with specific purposes or identifiable goals. In Acts 13:2 fasting accompanied the ordination of Barnabas and Saul to be missionaries. In Acts 14:23 fasting and prayer accompanied the ordination of elders. One young minister shared with me how he had fasted regularly since the birth of his first child in seeking spiritual guidance as a parent. That seems altogether right and proper.

Is there a spiritual need in your life? God might be

honored by your pursuing the fulfillment of that need not only through prayer but through fasting. While that may not always be the case, you and I should always be open to it. J. Oswald Sanders shares this illustration:

> In the early days of the China Inland Mission, Dr.J. Hudson Taylor and his colleagues had reached the decision to ask God for seventy new missionaries – an almost unprecedented missionary petition in 1881. With a group of fellow missionaries, a day of united prayer and fasting was held. 'On the morning of our fast day,' wrote one participant, 'the Holy Spirit seemed so to fill several of us, that each felt (as we found in private conversation afterwards) that we could not bear any more and live.' The subjective blessing that was experienced by those who prayed was not the only result. God answered their prayers and gave the seventy workers.[89]

THE PRACTICE OF FASTING

I want to once again make it clear that while Jesus fasted and commended fasting in His teaching, He never made it a rite of the Kingdom. Indeed, some of Jesus' conversations, in and of themselves, would suggest His disdain for the discipline of fasting:

> Then the disciples of John came to Him, saying, "Why do we and the Pharisees fast, but Your disciples do not fast?" And Jesus said to them, 'The attendants of the bridegroom cannot mourn, as long as the bridegroom is with them, can they? But the days will come when the bridegroom is taken away from them, and then they will fast. But no one puts a patch of unshrunk cloth on an old garment; for the patch pulls away from the garment, and a worse tear results. Nor do men put new wine into

old wineskins; otherwise the wineskins burst, and the wine pours out, and the wineskins are ruined; but they put new wine into fresh wineskins, and both are preserved" (Matt. 9:14-17).

On another occasion Jesus said:

For John came neither eating nor drinking, and they say, "He has a demon!" The Son of Man came eating and drinking, and they say, "Behold, a gluttonous man and a drunkard, a friend of tax-gatherers and sinners!" Yet wisdom is vindicated by her deeds (Matt. 11:18-19).

Jesus time with His disciples on earth was characterized as a time of joy, of feasting, of celebration. However Jesus said, "The days will come when the bridegroom is taken away from them, and then they will fast" (Matt. 9:15). These are the days for fasting, these days between the ascension and the bodily, visible return of our Lord from heaven. These words are prophetic and the early Christians fulfilled them as have so many saintly men and women across the years. Where are the Christians who will fulfill them today? Arthur Wallis writes, "Fasting is a God-appointed means for the flowing of His grace and power that we can afford to neglect no longer."[90]

The primary guideline as to the practice of fasting is found in the text with which we began. In Matthew 6, Jesus taught that the attitude or spirit with which we approached fasting was all important. It is not to be done for show or for the approval of men but for the pleasure and approval of God.

As to the length of a fast, it most often lasted only one

day in the Bible. On three occasions a fast lasted 40 days. Moses, Elijah, and Jesus all fasted for forty days. Contrary to what many might think, a 40 day fast would be physically possible for most relatively healthy people, although I'm certainly not advocating that you start there or even that you set that as a goal.

There are also dangers in fasting. From a physical standpoint, diabetics, expectant mothers, and heart patients should not fast without approval of a physician. As great a danger, however, is the problem of spiritual hypocrisy or spiritual pride which can easily enter in. Remember the Pharisee Jesus condemned in Luke 18 proudly prayed, "I fast twice a week" (Luke 18:12). Another danger is that of legalism. This is a danger in all the disciplines but perhaps more with fasting than with any of the others because it is such a physical thing and can easily be done without spiritual intent or understanding. Having done so it is also easy to try to bind it on someone else. Properly understood, motivated, and practiced I certainly commend it to you. But neither I nor anyone else has the right to bind it on you.

Fasting will take on far greater significance and bring far greater benefits to your life if it is accompanied by repentance, and the asking of God's forgiveness and also accompanied by prayer directed toward a specific need or purpose. Also fasting can be the occasion for very meaningful personal worship of the Lord.

Thus far our thoughts have been centered on abstaining from food. However, Foster's definition, "the voluntary denial of an otherwise normal function for the sake of intense spiritual activity," could take in far more than food. As a matter of fact, there may be many types of fasts far more beneficial to some of us than fasting from food. One such fast is even suggested in Scripture. Paul raised the issue of a married couple abstaining from sex for spiritual purposes:

> Stop depriving one another, except by agreement for a time that you may devote yourselves to prayer, and come together again lest Satan tempt you because of your lack of self-control (I Cor. 7:5).

Notice that Paul gave three guidelines. First it was to be by mutual agreement. Next, it was to be brief so as not to bring unnecessary temptation. And finally, the couple was to devote themselves to prayer. Once again there is purpose even in this fast.

Richard Foster wrote an excellent article in the TSF Bulletin of November – December 1983 in which he suggested yet other non-food fasts. There is fasting from people, the discipline of solitude or spending time alone which we considered in Chapter 6. There is fasting from the media. One of the delights of my life is vacationing in Wyoming. The cabins where we stay have no radio nor TV. What a wonderful change of pace that is and how it enhances your time spent with God. Along that same line, Foster suggests fasting from the telephone. The telephone is a wonderful servant if we do not allow it to control us. There is nothing that says you have to answer it, you know. Foster also recommends fasting from conversation. Bonhoeffer wrote that when the tongue is under authority "much that is unnecessary remains unsaid, but the essential and the helpful thing can be said in a few words."[91]

Though he suggests others, I want to mention just one other fast which Foster mentions, fasting from a consumer culture. He writes, "We will discover times when we can fast from our gluttonous, comfortable consumer culture. For our soul's sake, we need times when we can be among Christ's favorites: the broken, the bruised, the dispossessed – not to preach to them, but to learn from them."[92]

Perhaps you can think of other fasts which might benefit you even more. What do you need to deny yourself in order to carry out some intense spiritual activity?

When you fast, and notice I said "when," not "if," I believe you will find the following five questions extremely helpful in making sure your fast honors the Lord.

> 1. Am I confident that this desire to fast is God-given? Would He have me undertake a normal or just a partial fast?
> 2. Are my motives right? Is there any hidden desire to impress others?
> 3. What are my spiritual objectives in this fast?
> 4. Do my objectives tend to be self-centered? Is my desire for personal blessing balanced by genuine concern for others?
> 5. Am I determined above all else to minister to the Lord in this fast?[93]

CONCLUSION

In John chapter four, the disciples had gone into the city of Sychar to buy food while Jesus rested at Jacob's

Well. There he met and ministered to the woman of Samaria who had had five husbands and was living with a man who was not her husband. He revealed Himself to her as the Messiah in one of the most meaningful dialogues recorded in Scripture. In the meantime the disciples returned with food and when the woman went hurrying off to town to tell the people she had met the Messiah, the disciples tried to get Him to eat. Jesus' response puzzled the disciples, "I have food to eat that you do not know about" (John 4:32). Now no one had come and given Him physical food but He went on to explain. "My food is to do the will of Him who sent Me, and to accomplish His work" (John 4:34).

What I want you to see is that fasting is not just giving up food . . . or even sex, people, media, the telephone, conversation or whatever. Fasting is giving it up for a time that you might better do the will of God. Fasting as with the other disciplines is not an end in itself but a means to the end of glorifying God.

I hope you'll try it. Pray for God to impress the need upon you. Search the Scriptures further on the subject. Begin with just a 24 hour period. You might want to covenant with a friend to fast on a certain day. Don't be ashamed of your fast, but don't boast of it either. And as you fast from physical food be sure to feast on Christ and His Word.

The ultimate hope of the Church lies in the promise of the reappearance of our Lord from heaven. He said, "I will come again." He taught us that while He, the Bridegroom, is gone it is proper that we fast. Fasting in this age of the absent Bridegroom is in anticipation of

His coming again. Hopefully it will not be long before we hear the midnight cry, "Behold, the bridegroom! Come out to meet Him!"(Matt. 25:6). The day of fasting will be over when we see Him. The time for fasting and preparation is now!

THOUGHT QUESTIONS:

1. Why did Jesus not make fasting obligatory?

2. Can fasting ever be spiritually harmful?

3. How do you think fasting may reveal what controls your life? What might you need to fast from besides food?

4. What should a Christian's attitude be while fasting?

5. Why do you think so many Christians find fasting so unattractive?

6. How would you account for the lack of teaching on and practice of fasting in the twentieth century?

7. What are the benefits of fasting if the act has no inherent spiritual merit?

8. Why had the practice of fasting become something to be called into question among the Pharisees of Jesus day? How could it become such today?

9. What do you consider the most important guidelines in regard to the discipline of fasting?

ASSIGNMENTS:

Identify and list needs, goals, or specific purposes in your life for which fasting coupled with prayer could be properly practiced.

Write a short paragraph describing your thinking on fasting at this point. Especially note any changes in your thinking brought about by this study.

SCRIPTURE REFERENCES:

Matt. 6:16-18	Zech. 7:5	I Cor. 9:25-27
Luke 2:37	Matt. 17:21	Acts 13:2
Matt. 4:2	Ezra 8:23	Acts 14:23
Acts 9:9	Jonah 3:10	Matt. 9:14-17
Ezra 10:6	Phil. 3:19	Matt. 11:18-19
Daniel 10:3	II Tim. 2:22	Luke 18:12
Col. 2:20-23	Titus 2:12	I Cor. 7:5
Rom. 14:17	I Peter 2:11	John 4:32-34
I Cor. 8:8	Rom. 13:14	Matt. 25:6

RECOMMENDED READING

God's Chosen Fast by Arthur Wallis
Fasting: What The Bible Teaches by Jerry Falwell
Fasting: A Neglected Discipline by David R. Smith
Fasting Changed My Life by Andy Anderson

PASSAGES TO READ WHILE FASTING:

Isaiah 58:1-14	Daniel 2:1-21	Psalm 51:1-19
Matt. 17:1-21	Esther 1-10	John 21:1-21
I Samuel 1:1-2:11		

QUOTABLE QUOTES:

"It is only in a life of moderation and temperance and self-denial that there will be the heart or the strength to pray much."

–Andrew Murray, from WITH CHRIST IN THE
SCHOOL OF PRAYER

"The central idea in fasting is the voluntary denial of an otherwise normal function for the sake of intense spiritual activity."

–Richard Foster

PRAYER:

"O Lord, who for our sake didst fast forty days and forty nights, give us grace to use such abstinence that, our flesh being subdued to the spirit, we may ever obey Thy godly motions in righteousness, and true holiness, to Thy honor and glory, who livest and reignest with the Father and the Holy Spirit, one God, world without end. Amen."

–Anonymous from PRAYER POWER UNLIMITED

Chapter Nine

GROWING THROUGH PERSONAL WORSHIP

IT HAPPENS! Your spirit touches the Spirit of God and you know the reality of genuine worship, real praise and adoration. Years ago I was sitting in an early morning session for preachers at a North American Christian Convention. A soloist was singing "How Great Thou Art" in a rich, baritone voice. How many times had I heard that song? Hundreds of times? Probably. But when he came to the part that says, "And when I think that God, His Son not sparing, sent Him to die, I scarce can take it in; that on the cross MY BURDEN gladly bearing, He bled and died to take away MY SIN. Then sings my soul, my savior God to Thee, how great Thou art!" And all of a sudden it became personal and the tears began to flow and my spirit reached out to the Spirit of God in genuine worship and praise for who He is and all He has done for me.

We were vacationing in Ogunquit, Maine. There is this fantastic one mile walk that winds along the edge of the cliffs where the pounding surf of the Atlantic meets the shore. I had gotten up early and taken my Bible along as I walked the path just before dawn. I made my way out onto some rocks jutting out into the sea where I sat awestruck as the sun rose bright orange, seemingly from the midst of the sea. The seagulls frolicked nearby. The sound of the waves crashing against the rocks filled the fresh morning air. Suddenly I found myself singing and praising the Lord from the depths of my being.

I could describe many similar experiences: morning devotions in a park overlooking the Mississippi River in Keokuk, Iowa; sunset in the Grand Tetons of Wyoming; some especially meaningful worship services; and yes, kneeling at the entrance to the empty tomb in a garden just outside the walled city of Jerusalem. In each case the meaning of I Peter 1:8 has been experienced:

> And though you have not seen Him, you love Him, and though you do not see Him now, but believe in Him, you greatly rejoice with joy inexpressible and full of glory.

However, such experiences are not to be the isolated instances of happenstance. Surely God intends for all of His children to make personal worship a regular part of life.

There is a great deal of overlap in the disciplines that we have been discussing. Thus, if we truly pray as we ought, if we study and meditate on God's Word, and we keep a spiritual journal recording our walk with God, and we have a daily quiet time and we practice the discipline of fasting, it is altogether likely that we will have worshiped. But worship, and we are speaking primarily of personal rather than corporate worship, should not only not be something we happen upon from time to time; it should not be the mere byproduct of the other disciplines either. Worship should be intentional or purposeful as well. For God is both worthy of and desirous of our praise.

Webster defines worship as: "worthiness, repute, respect, reverence paid to a divine being." J. Oswald Sanders says, "Worship, then, is the loving ascription of praise to God for what He is, both in Himself and in His ways. It is the bowing of the innermost spirit in deep humility and reverence before Him."[94]

Worship begins with an attitude of the heart, an attitude we see in King David as reflected in His words in Psalm 63:

> O God, Thou art my God; I shall seek Thee earnestly; My soul thirsts for Thee, my flesh yearns for Thee, in a dry and weary land where there is no water. Thus I have beheld Thee in the sanctuary . . . (Psa. 63:1-11).

David was hungry and thirsty for God. Another Psalmist puts it this way:

> As the deer pants for the water brooks, so my soul pants for Thee, O God. My soul thirsts for God, for the living

175

God. When shall I come and appear before God? (Psa. 42:1-2).

We try to substitute programs, methods, organizations, and gimmicks for longing after God. But true worship beings with a longing for God. In Psalm 63 David lists several things that promote such a longing and thus promote true personal worship.

PREPARATION FOR WORSHIP

In verse two, David says, "Thus I have beheld Thee in the sanctuary, to see Thy power and Thy glory." The key words are "beheld" and "see." Now David didn't see the Lord with his physical eyes but He did see Him in his mind and his spirit. If we are going to practice the discipline of personal worship, we must learn to center our minds on the Lord. Use your mind to see God's power and glory. Contemplate His majesty. It is always helpful to me to read one of the great passages describing Him like Revelation 1 where He is described in such powerful symbolism as hair white like wool, eyes like a flame of fire, feet like burnished bronze, a voice like the sound of many waters, a two-edged sword protruding from His mouth, and His face like the sun shining in all its strength. We need to see the Lord in all His powerful attributes symbolized by such language: His eternal nature, His ability to see into the soul of a man, His judgment upon sin, His majesty, the power of His Word, and His personal beauty and glory. Again, we're talking about seeing or beholding the Lord through the eyes of faith.

In John MacArthur's book, *The Ultimate Priority*, he tells of a report in the *Chicago Tribune* of a New Mexico woman who was frying tortillas when she noticed that the skillet burns on the tortilla resembled the face of Jesus. MacArthur writes:

Excited, she showed it to her husband and neighbors, and they all agreed that there was a face etched on the tortilla and that it truly bore a resemblance to Jesus.

So the woman went to her priest to have the tortilla blessed. She testified that the tortilla had changed her life, and her husband agreed that she had been a more peaceful, happy, submissive wife since the tortilla had arrived. The priest, not accustomed to blessing tortillas, was somewhat reluctant but agreed to do it.

The woman took the tortilla home, put it in a glass case with piles of cotton to make it look like it was floating on clouds, built a special altar for it, and opened the little shrine to visitors. Within a few months, more than eight thousand people came to the shrine of JESUS OF THE TORTILLA, and all of them agreed that the face in the burn marks on the tortilla was the face of Jesus (except for one reporter who said he thought it looked like former heavyweight champion Leon Spinks).[95]

It is important that we remember that the object of our worship is the living Lord. It is important for us to see Him in all His attributes for He is a God of love, wisdom, grace, and mercy. He is kind, patient, intelligent, holy, and true. He is sovereign, unchangeable, majestic, omnipresent, omniscient, and omnipotent. The list of His attributes goes on and on. It would be helpful just to take the time to make such a list.

If we really center our minds on the person of Christ, it will almost inevitably lead us to a confession of our own sinfulness and weakness. Do you remember Isaiah's experience? When he saw the Lord sitting upon His throne and the seraphim proclaiming His holiness, then Isaiah said:

> Woe is me, for I am ruined! Because I am a man of unclean lips, and I live among a people of unclean lips; for my eyes have seen the King, the Lord of Hosts (Isa. 6:5).

To enter into genuine worship will bring us face to face with the holiness of God and cannot help but underscore our own unrighteousness.

Lynne Hybels retells the story of Quasimodo, the hunchback of Notre Dame. This poor man had been deformed from birth but when he poured out his heart to the beautiful gypsy, Esmeralda, he saw himself as more hideous and grotesque than ever before.

> I never realized my ugliness till now. When I compare myself with you, I pity myself indeed, poor unhappy monster that I am! I must seem to you like some awful beast, eh? You – you are a sunbeam, a drop of dew, a bird's song! As for me, I am something frightful, neither man nor beast – a nondescript object, more hard, shapeless, and more trodden under foot than a pebble![96]

It is important in personal worship that we see ourselves for what we are, sinners, desperately in need of God's saving grace.

I believe it is also important that we approach worship with what Richard Foster calls a "holy expectancy." As you recall those special moments in your own life in which you stumbled into the presence of divine majesty, almost by chance, surely you should eagerly desire similar experiences of the glorious, gracious presence of the living God. The only way I know to cultivate such an expectancy is to live each hour of each day in an awareness of His presence. Let me strongly recommend that you read the little book, *The Practice Of The Presence Of God* by Brother Lawrence. Because he knew God's presence in the kitchen where he worked, he could expect His presence in his personal devotional life as well. Lawrence wrote, "I cannot imagine how religious persons can live satisfied without the practice of the presence of God."[97] Are you aware of God's presence at your desk in the office, or there on the assembly line, or in the laundry room? Do you realize He is your companion when you go shopping or on a picnic? We need to cultivate the expectancy of encountering the living God in our personal worship by being more aware of His presence, His power, and His blessing every hour of every day.

Many professing Christians live out their work-a-day world with very little difference from their non-Christian counterparts. We get accustomed to doing things in our own strength and wisdom and the only difference in our lives and those of others about us is a slightly more sensitized moral awareness. Many times there isn't even that. What a difference it would make if we were sensitive to God's presence in every conversation, every transaction, and every relationship. And if there were a sense of the divine in all of that, I can guarantee you it would overflow into a much more meaningful experience with the Lord when we enter into a specific time of personal worship. Preparation for worship includes seeing the Lord, seeing ourselves in relation to Him, and expecting His presence in our worship even as He is present with us in all that we do.

THE PRACTICE OF WORSHIP

In verses three through eight of Psalm 63, we get some insights into David's practice of worship. I'm not suggesting some sort of mechanical formula. Foster rightly points out, "We can use all the right techniques and methods, we can have the best possible liturgy, but we have not worshiped the Lord until Spirit touches spirit."[98] But there were certain elements to David's worship that are important elements in ours.

The first of these is the giving of praise to God. Having pictured God, David gave praise to Him for who and what He was. "My lips will praise Thee. So I will bless Thee as long as I live; I will lift up my hands in Thy name" (vs. 3-4). David speaks of praise, not in a corporate sense, but in a personal sense. There was personal praise, with his lips, his heart, and his hands. Praise, as I understand it, is the expressing of adoration to God without the mention of yourself. We tell the Lord what we love and adore about Him. We praise His name, His character, His attributes, His acts, and His Word.

And let me tell you, God loves the praise of His people. You and I who were made in His image love praise, even when it is undeserved. But there is no praise you can offer to God of which He is undeserving. Furthermore, it is right that we bring Him praise for it is praise that is the sacrifice He desires in this new age of grace. The Hebrew writer said it so well:

> Through Him (Christ), let us continually offer up a sacrifice of praise to God, that is, the fruit of lips that give thanks to His name (Heb. 13:15).

Now if you want to learn how to give praise, I would suggest a study of the Psalms. The Psalms are filled with exhortations to praise the Lord. Many begin with those very words, "Praise the Lord!" The Psalms also demonstrate that praise can be expressed in many different ways. We can praise God by singing, by shouting, by dancing, by clapping our hands, by raising our hands, by kneeling down, by lifting our heads, and even by laughing. God loves a holy laugh. Psalm 150 gives a long list of instruments with which we can praise the Lord. Actually there is no end to the ways in which we can offer up praise. Oh, I know, some of us say we're just too inhibited to be at all demonstrative in praising the Lord. Yet I've watched enough ballgames to know that our inhibition is somewhat selective.

Men, do you remember when you were pursuing that lovely lady who became your wife? Do you remember how you told her of your love? You also spoke of her beauty and how she was the most wonderful woman in the world. It probably wouldn't hurt any husband to take a refresher course in that regard. And you ladies told that guy how handsome or at least how cute he was. You told him he was the smartest or the strongest or the most talented guy you'd ever known. Now even at the time you knew some of that was hype – although that didn't keep the other person from enjoying it. But again, you can't exaggerate about God. You can't flatter God. Everything good you can say is true – only more so. Perhaps you have never really told God how you feel about Him. Let me suggest that you get off to yourself and spend some time just telling God how great He is and how much you love Him and how thankful you are that He loves you and cares for you.

Another way David worshiped was through meditation. "When I remember Thee on my bed, I meditate on Thee in the night watches, for Thou hast been my help" (vs. 6). Having devoted an entire chapter to meditation, we won't deal extensively with it here. However, David not only pictured the Lord and praised Him, he focused his mind on Him and His Word even in the night. Again, we can better understand this if we relate it to romance. When my wife Jan and I were going together, I kept her picture right on my desk at college. And often, when I should have been studying, I was looking at her picture and thinking about her, wanting to be with her, and planning our life together. Worship is like that, but the Lord is the focus of our thoughts. When you go to bed at night instead of warm milk, Sominex, or counting sheep, cultivate the habit of meditating on the Lord and His Word. Think on what He had done for you. Picture Him as the One who can meet your need now. Meditation is certainly a part of worship.

Notice that David also specifically mentions singing as a part of his worship experience. In verses seven and eight he says, "For Thou hast been my help, and in the shadow of Thy wings I sing for joy. My soul clings to Thee; Thy right hand upholds me." David reflected on God's help and protection and he expressed his spontaneous worship in song. Singing is certainly not unique to Christianity, but from a Scriptural standpoint, it is a very important element both in our worship and the expression of our faith. At least forty-one times we are commanded in the Psalms to "sing unto the Lord." Paul tells us to "be filled with the Spirit," and then goes on to say, "Speaking to one another in psalms and hymns and spiritual songs, singing and making melody with your heart to the Lord" (Eph. 5:19). Similarly he writes in Colossians, "Let the word of Christ richly dwell within you, with all wisdom teaching and admonishing one another with psalms and hymns and spiritual songs, singing with thankfulness in your hearts to God" (Col. 3:16).

What would our corporate worship be without singing? Much of it would be no more nor less than a Bible lecture. But music transforms all that we do. It does teach and admonish but it also aids our spirit in reaching out to the Spirit of God. Music, more than any other single element of corporate worship, aids me in being ready to worship and aids me in expressing my praise to the Lord. Does it not stand to reason that it is equally important in personal worship?

Often I've used recorded music to prepare my heart

and to encourage me to worship. Many is the time that I've sat alone listening to Sandi Patty singing "We Shall Behold Him" and in my mind I have beheld Him in all of His glory, and I've longed to see Him in His visible, bodily return, and my heart has overflowed with praise to Him. I also have several praise chorus tapes that I not only listen to but sing along with. Each day in my quiet time I sing to the Lord. And by the way, I believe He hears me the way I want to sound rather than the way you would judge me.

There was an Aussie at Trinity while I was studying there who always sang in the shower, but he always sang to the Lord. Each time I roomed in the dorm I only looked forward to hearing him sing; not because he had a tremendous voice, nor simply because I loved his accent, nor even because I loved to hear his stories of missionary service for the Lord, but because his singing was so obviously genuine praise. The way a man sings can say a lot about his walk with God. Cultivate that practice. We are rich today in that there are so many excellent praise choruses that have been written. A book of such choruses is a very helpful tool in personal worship.

How did David worship the Lord? He did it through offering up praise or adoration from his lips. He expressed that praise not just verbally but physically, in this case through lifting up his hands. He meditated on the Lord and on all He had done for him. Another specific expression of worship was through song. I would certainly not suggest that this is the final word on the practice of personal worship. But at least it gives you a place to start. Let me suggest you start today.

THE PRODUCT OF WORSHIP

In verses 9-11 of Psalm 63, David speaks of a difficult time in his life. It is most probable that this was the time of Absalom's rebellion. David refers to himself when he says, "The King will rejoice in God." Even in the midst of personal difficulty he would rejoice as he worshiped God. So it is today, if we learn to worship the Lord in the good times, we'll be able to seek His strength in the difficult times.

Now the product of all this is many-faceted, but the most important facet is that it blesses God. Not only does it please Him and make Him happy, but it glorifies or honors him as well. Ruth Myers tells of the death of her first husband, Dean Denler. In those final days just before cancer took his life, praise took on a new importance to him. He told Ruth that he would soon be praising God throughout eternity, but that only here on earth could he bring joy to God by praising Him in the midst of his difficulty and pain. She said he simply made his hospital room a place of praise. At his funeral a close friend stated, "His room became a sanctuary, his bed a pulpit, and all who came to comfort him were blessed."[99] No, his personal worship of the living Lord did not result in the healing of his earthly body, but it did bring spiritual refreshment and encouragement into his life and it honored and glorified God in death even as he had in his life. And while that may be an extreme

185

example, our genuine worship always honors and glorifies God.

However, even as personal worship blesses God, it is also true that you are blessed. I think back to an incident in 1963 when I first recognized something of this fact. I had just recently rededicated my life to Christ and He had turned my whole life around. I was in my '59 Ford heading for Joplin, Missouri, to enroll at Ozark Bible College. I can remember it well. I was singing to the Lord with all my might when I felt the steering wheel begin to jerk and then came the all-too-familiar "thump, thump, thump." I got out and took a look at my now totally flat tire, opened the trunk to get out the spare and discovered that it too was flat. I was about a mile from Carthage, Missouri, so I took out the spare and started rolling it westward toward the nearest service station. As I rolled it along, I began to sing. I wasn't even conscious of what I was singing at first, but it finally dawned on me that I was singing, "Be not dismayed what'ere betide; God will take care of you." I had to stop singing because I began laughing. If you would have known me before, this was an entirely ludicrous picture. Only months before my blood pressure would already have skyrocketed, my mind would have been filled with anger, and the words on my lips would not have been words of praise. Yet how much better off was the new John Caldwell than the old would have been.

It's true that the old John Caldwell still rises from the grave from time to time, at least in regard to anger and anxiety. But I've come far enough to know beyond any shadow of a doubt that I'm far better off just praising the Lord. Recently in rushing to make a 12:05 Sunday afternoon flight after a late dismissal of our second morning worship service, I first got a speeding ticket. Now running later than ever, my insides are tied in knots because I "had to make that flight!" When I got there I was on time but the flight wasn't because there were mechanical difficulties. Finally I began to practice what I preach. I told the Lord it was in His hands and that if I were to make it to Oklahoma City on time, He'd have to take care of it. I relaxed in Him, praising Him for His power to provide. Even though my flight arrived in Chicago for my connecting flight forty-five minutes late and the next flight was to leave in less than five minutes, I not only made the flight, I got to go first class, and my luggage got to Oklahoma City at the same time I did. That, my friends, is a modern-day miracle!

Some time back it happened again. I was up for jury duty. I really don't mind doing my part but the timing was incredibly bad. Not only was Jan's mother at the point of death but I had so much work piled up that I didn't know how I could ever dig my way out. But I reported for jury selection, praying that the Lord would get me excused. Imagine my disappointment when in spite of my doing everything short of lying to get excused, I was seated as a juror. Why hadn't God said "yes" to my prayer? After the jury was impaneled and instructed, we were sent to lunch while the attorneys made some pre-testimony arguments. Upon returning from our free lunch, we were returned to the courtroom where the judge told us that for only the second time in all the years he had served as a judge, the defendant had looked at the selected jury and decided to plead guilty instead of taking his chances with us. Furthermore, since we had officially been seated as jurors, it was as though we had sat for an entire trial and were therefore no longer eligible to be called for jury duty. You see, God's ways are always better than ours. I'm a slow learner but that lesson is finally sinking in. Instead of allowing myself to get caught in a downward spiral of negative thoughts I'm learning more and more to focus my attention on God's power, His grace, and His ability to intervene in any situation and bring good from it, even though I may not always readily see that good. Personal worship blesses you.

Finally, personal worship changes you. Richard Foster even goes so far as to say, "If worship does not change us, it has not been worship. To stand before the Holy One of eternity is to change . . . If worship does not propel us into great obedience, it has not been worship. Just as worship begins in holy expectancy, it ends in holy obedience."[100] Lynne Hybels says, "True worship transforms the worshipper. That is not, of course, its primary function. Its primary function is to honor God. But the result of true worship – the inevitable result – is the transformation of the worshipper."[101] Dr. R.A. Torrey, the great revivalist, said that an utter transformation came about in his life when he learned not just to pray but to truly worship – asking nothing from God, seeking nothing from God, but focused on and satisfied with God.[102] Let me urge you to enter into this discipline of personal worship which will not only bless and honor God, and not only bless your life, but totally transform your life.

CONCLUSION

J. Oswald Sanders tells the story of Scipio Africanus. [103] After a resounding victory in battle, he returned to Rome, riding in triumph, followed by hundreds of captives. As he made his way through the streets of the eternal city, he threw the spoils of war to the crowds that lined the way. Some of the people honored him because they were grateful for his gifts; some because he had turned back an invading army and kept them safe; but there were others who gave little thought to their personal benefit, they simply praised the qualities of the victor – his courage, resourcefulness, and liberality. It was that last group that best represented the highest aspect of worship.

Certainly we should worship the Lord because He has provided so graciously for us and we are grateful. We should worship because He has provided even for the salvation of our souls, for our redemption. It is even right that we adore Him because that is best for us, the very practice of worship benefits us. However, let us never forget that our Lord is worthy of our worship just because of who He is. A favorite poem of mine written by Francis Xavier in the early fifteen hundreds expresses this idea:

My God, I love Thee; not because

I hope for heaven thereby,
Nor yet because who love Thee not
    Are lost eternally.
Thou, O my Jesus, Thou didst me
    Upon the cross embrace;
For me didst bear the nails, and spear,
    And manifold disgrace,
And griefs and torments numberless,
    And sweat of agony;
Yea, death itself; and all for me
    Who was thine enemy.
Then why, O blessed Jesu Christ,
    Should I not love Thee well?
Not for the sake of winning heaven,
    Nor of escaping hell;
Not from the hope of gaining aught,
    Not seeking a reward;
But as Thyself hast loved me,
    O ever-loving Lord.
So would I love Thee, dearest Lord,
    And in Thy praise will sing;
Solely because Thou art my God,
    And my most loving King.

Don't you love Him for who He is? Picture Him. Praise Him. Meditate on Him and His Word. Sing to Him. Adore Him. He'll be honored, glorified and blessed. However, you will be blessed abundantly as well. The practice of worship on a personal level would revolutionize many a Christian's spiritual life.

THOUGHT QUESTIONS:

1. In what ways will worship encourage spiritual growth?

2. Have you had some especially meaningful wor-

ship experience? What made it so special?

3. What are some ways you could assure a more consistent practice of personal worship?

4. Why do you believe worship is so important to God?

5. What are some of the benefits of worship for God?

6. What are some of the benefits of worship for you?

7. Why should we praise God even in our difficulties?

8. What are two or three of the things you most appreciate about our Lord? Praise Him for them right now.

9. What are a few of the most significant blessings you've experienced in life? Praise God for them.

10. What are some of your greatest disappointments in life? Can you still praise God?

ASSIGNMENTS:

Write out your own psalm of praise. You can do it!

Make a list of God's attributes. God is holy, righteous, just, loving . . . How many attributes can you name?

Read Psalm 100, 103, 104, 147, 150; I Chronicles 16:8-36.

SCRIPTURE REFERENCES:

I Peter 1:8	Revelation 1:10-20	Psalm 150:1-6
Psalm 63:1-11	Isaiah 6:5	Ephesians 5:19
Psalm 42:1-2	Hebrews 13:15	Colossians 3:16

RECOMMENDED READING:

The Joy Of Personal Worship by Lynne Hybels
Praise: A Door To God's Presence by Warren & Ruth
   Myers
Praise & Worship by Anne Murcheson
The Practice Of The Presence Of God by Brother
   Lawrence
Sweet Hour of Prayer by Don DeWelt

PRAYER:

"Eternal Father of my soul, let my first thought today be of You, let my first impulse be to worship You, let my first speech be Your name, let my first action be to kneel in prayer, Amen."
                                        –from A DIARY OF PRIVATE PRAYER
                                                       by John Baillie

TEN ACTS OF PRAISE

1. Laughter (Psa. 126:1-2)
2. The singing mouth (Psa. 89:1)
3. The bent knee (Psa. 95:6)
4. The bowed head (Neh. 8:5-6)
5. The clapping hand (Psa. 47:1)
6. The shouting voice (Psa. 98:4)
7. The uplifted hands (II Chron. 6:13)
8. The dancing feet (Exod. 15:20)
9. The grounded face (Job 1:20)
10. The uplifted head (Psa. 3:3)

Chapter Ten

GROWING THROUGH MINISTRY

Our emphasis has been on the inner life, on the development of Christian disciplines for spiritual growth. Again and again we've used Jesus as an example, for it was He who taught us to pray; He who showed us the importance of time alone with God; He who showed us how important it is that we study God's Word; and He who modeled the discipline of fasting for us. It was also Jesus who taught us that no amount of outward performance is of any positive consequence if it is not properly motivated from within. However, if you were to ask Jesus why He came to earth, He would not say that He came to pray, fast, or study God's Word.

Instead He would answer:

My food is to DO the will of Him who sent Me, and to ACCOMPLISH His work (John 4:34).

Or He would say,

For the Son of Man has come to SEEK and to SAVE that which was lost (Luke 19:10).

And we would also hear Him say,

Whoever wishes to become great among you shall be your servant; and whoever wishes to be first among you shall be slave of all. For even the Son of Man did not come to be served, but to serve, and to give His life a ransom for many (Mark 10:43-45).

As we come to this final chapter on spiritual disciplines, it is important that we be reminded that the inner life does not exist as an end in itself but as a means to the end of doing the will of God and thus glorifying Him. A devotional life that does not result in Christian ministry is not true devotion. We must not fall into the trap of believing that the outward life is unimportant. We should, however, understand that an outward life of service, motivated by an intimate, close, personal walk with the Lord, is what pleases Him. It is not the inward life versus the outward life or devotion versus ministry at issue. God is concerned about both the inward and the outward. He wants both devotion and ministry. But the outward life is to be motivated by inward spirituality and our ministry or service is to be prompted by devotion. That's what He wants.

This book grew out of my own personal need for inner, spiritual growth and an awareness of such a need on the part of the church both local and universal. When I wrote to dozens of Christian leaders across the country asking for their input, I found my evaluation almost universally affirmed. However, one response, from a very gifted pastor whom I've always admired, seemed to chastise my intended emphasis. In referring to those who have emphasized the devotional disciplines, he spoke of some "glaring inconsistencies between their inner lives and their outer walk." He went on to say:

> My conviction is that we deepen spiritually as we reach out evangelistically. Fascinating, isn't it, that Jesus didn't commission us to a life of Bible study, devotions, confession, journaling, etc., but to a life of making disciples . . . I have grown most, have walked most closely with the Lord, have enjoyed being a Christian most when I have been most involved in introducing others to Christ. It is evangelism more than anything else that has given the Spirit a chance to grow His fruit in me: love, joy, peace, patience, kindness, etc . . . Of course we must feed on His Word, meditate on its meaning, pray without ceasing, and so on – but in conjunction with and seldom if ever apart from reaching out in love to those whom I would do anything to rescue.[104]

Again, it is not one or the other but both/and. However, what this brother said is true. If we only ate and didn't exercise it would not be a healthy situation. The Dead Sea will not sustain life because the Jordan River flows into it but no water flows out. So it is with the Christian life. The Christian who develops all the inward disciplines we've discussed but who does not use the resulting spiritual power for ministry is simply not in the will of God. However, the Christian who does not practice such disciplines will not have the spiritual power to accomplish what God would have him accomplish.

I want us to put everything in balance. I hope you will grow in your spiritual life. But what are you going to do with the added spiritual vitality? There's no doubt about what God wants you to do with it. He wants you to use it in ministry – that is in serving others in His name. Let's look at three aspects of that ministry: our model for ministry, our motivation for ministry, and our method of ministry.

OUR MODEL FOR MINISTRY

Of course our model is Jesus Christ, Himself. Because of what Jesus was inwardly, He was a SERVANT outwardly. Because He was totally surrendered to the will of the Father and because He loved man, he was committed to serving. Devotion to God and love for man is demonstrated in serving others.

Jesus modeled that when at the Last Supper He heard His disciples arguing about who was the greatest. First Jesus taught them a very important principle:

The kings of the Gentiles lord it over them; and those who have authority over them are called 'Benefactors.' But not so with you, but let him who is the greatest among you become as the youngest, and the leader as the servant. For who is greater, the one who reclines at table, or the one who serves? Is it not the one who reclines at table? But I am among you as the one who serves (Luke 22:25-27).

Then Jesus demonstrated the truth of what He taught. He got up from the table, laid His outer clothing aside, wrapped a towel around His waist, poured water into a basin, knelt down, and began to wash the feet of His disciples and dried them with the towel. Then Jesus explained the significance of what He had done.

> And so when He had washed their feet, and taken His garments, and reclined at table again, He said to them, 'Do you know what I have done to you? You call me Teacher, and Lord; and you are right; for so I am. If I then, the Lord and the Teacher, washed your feet, you also ought to wash one another's feet. For I gave you an example that you also should do as I did to you. Truly, truly, I say to you, a slave is not greater than his master; neither one who is sent greater than the one who sent him. If you know these things, you are blessed if you do them (John 13:12-17).

As Ray Stedman points out, what Christ did was actually a parable of His entire life. Paul summarizes what Christ did in Philippians 2:5-11:

> Have this attitude in yourselves which was also in Christ Jesus, who, although He existed in the form of God, did not regard equality with God a thing to be grasped, but emptied Himself, taking the form of a bond-servant, and being made in the likeness of men. And being found in appearance as a man, He humbled Himself by becoming obedient to the point of death, even death on a cross. Therefore also God highly exalted Him, and bestowed on Him the name which is above every name, that at the name of Jesus every knee should bow, of those who are in heaven, and on earth, and

under the earth, and that every tongue should confess that Jesus Christ is Lord, to the glory of God the Father.

John tells us that Jesus ROSE from supper as He had done in a far greater way when He left His throne of glory in preparation for coming into this world. John says HE LAID ASIDE HIS GARMENTS just as Paul tells us He emptied Himself of all outward manifestations of His deity and appeared on earth as a man among men. Next John says He GIRDED HIMSELF WITH A TOWEL. That is to say He took on the appearance of a servant. Paul says He "took the form of a bond-servant." And then John tells us that Jesus POURED WATER into a basin and began to wash the disciples' feet even as a few hours later He would pour out His blood that the sins of mankind might be washed away. The parable ends with Jesus PUTTING HIS GARMENTS BACK ON and returning to the table. In the same way, following His death, burial, and resurrection we know that Jesus ascended again to the right hand of the Father where He is once again clothed in glory. Stedman writes:

> There can be little doubt that here Jesus was deliberately working out a parable for the instruction of His disciples. He was dramatizing for them the character of His ministry. He was showing them by this means what He had come into the world to do, and what He would send them out to do.[105]

James Montgomery Boice contrasts what Jesus did as described in Philippians 2 and illustrated in John 13 with the analysis of Satan recorded in Isaiah 14:12-14.

Satan said, "I will go up. I will become like God. I will push God from His place." Jesus said, "I will go down. I will become like man. I will die to save him." This is one of the greatest, if not the greatest, contrasts of life – the contrast between Satan's way, which is also the way of the world, and God's way, embodied in Jesus Christ.[106]

Now, listen again to the words of Jesus in John 13:14-15:

You call me Teacher, and Lord; and you are right; for so I am. If I then, the Lord and the Teacher, washed your feet, you also ought to wash one another's feet. For I gave you an example that you also should do as I did to you.

Where does a life of Christian disciplines for spiritual growth lead? It leads you to your knees. It leads you into ministry. It leads you to become a servant. If that is not the result, then call it what you will, but genuine spiritual growth has not taken place, for spiritual growth makes us more and more like Jesus. Now all of this leads us to think about . . . .

OUR MOTIVATION FOR MINISTRY

The whole tension between an emphasis on the inner life and the outward performance has to do with the question of motivation. Jesus certainly approved of the good things which the Pharisees did but He faulted them for their improper motivation. We still struggle with the question of proper versus improper motivation in our personal ministry today.

Richard Foster has done an excellent job of analyzing

the improper motivations that still exist for ministry. He calls improperly motivated ministry, "self-righteous service." He makes nine observations.[107] First he says, "Self-righteous service comes through human effort." Is what we do motivated and empowered by the Spirit of God or the power of the flesh? I have to constantly ask myself that question. Next Foster observes, "Self-righteous service is impressed with the 'big deal'." That is to say, improperly motivated service is concerned about making an impression, attracting attention.

His next observation is related. "Self-righteous service requires external rewards." It needs praise, human applause and appreciation. While there is nothing wrong with such rewards, Jesus made it clear that if that is what we are seeking, we'll receive no further spiritual reward. A poem by Ruth Harms Calkin puts it all in perspective. It's entitled, "I Wonder."

> You know, Lord, how I serve You
> With great emotional fervor
> In the limelight.
> You know how eagerly I speak for You
> At a women's club.
> You know how I effervesce when I promote
> A fellowship group.
> You know my genuine enthusiasm
> At a Bible study.
>
> But how would I react, I wonder
> If You pointed to a basin of water
> And asked me to wash the calloused feet
> Of a bent and wrinkled old woman
> Day after day
> Month after month
> In a room where nobody saw
> And nobody knew.[108]

As a preacher it is flattering to speak to well over a thousand people each Lord's Day, to speak for major conventions, and to have to turn down many times more speaking engagements than you can take. Again, I have to ask myself if I could serve as gladly in some, small, out-of-the-way place where no one else would know I existed, if I knew it to be God's will. The same thing is true of every Christian. Oh, we all need affirmation. But could we, would we serve as gladly if no one knew? I'm glad there are many at Kingsway for whom the answer would be "Yes." When I went to church member Gloria Beck's hospital room, it looked like a greenhouse. I mentioned that to someone else who quickly responded, "It's because Gloria and Dave do so much for others." And it's true. They and so many others serve in so many ways without recognition, motivated only by a love for God and their fellow man.

Foster's fourth observation is, "Self-righteous service is highly concerned with results." Foster refers to the expectation of reciprocation and the heavy disappointment that comes when the other person does not respond in kind. "Self-righteous service picks and chooses whom to serve," says Foster. Sometimes improperly motivated ministry will serve the high and powerful because they can "do us more good" or it serves the down-and-outer to insure an image of humility. Jesus said we are to be "servant of all" (Mark 9:35).

Let me quickly list Foster's four additional observations. "Self-righteous service is affected by moods and whims." True service ministers when there is a need, not merely when we feel like serving. "Self-righteous service is temporary." Having done its part, it is content to let others take over while true service is a manner of life. "Self-righteous service is without sensitivity." Foster is talking about our determination to serve even when such service is neither wanted or needed. Finally, "Self-righteous service fractures community. In the final analysis, it centers in the glorification of the individual."

Having looked at improper motivation, let's turn our attention toward the positive and look at proper motivation. The whole thesis of this book has been that Christian people who are growing in their Christian lives, and thus becoming more and more like Jesus, will very naturally reflect that fact in doing what Jesus came to do – not to be ministered to but to minister and specifically to seek and to save the lost. That's why the Scriptures affirm again and again that while we are saved by faith we are judged according to our works. Our ministry to others is the outward evidence of a heart surrendered to the Lord. In Matthew twenty-five, the people who fed the hungry, gave drink to the thirsty, housed the wanderer, clothed the naked, visited the sick, and ministered to the imprisoned were not saved because they did those things. They did those things because they were in a right relationship with God. It is impossible to be in a right relationship with God and be unconcerned about the things that concern God. And the more we grow in our walk with the Lord, the more concerned we will be.

In her classic book, *The Christian's Secret Of A Happy Life*, Hannah Whitall Smith shares an illustration which powerfully pictures what I'm trying to say. She was visiting a home for the handicapped where the retarded were exercising to music. She said that they were making all sorts of awkward movements and only occasionally did their movements coincide with the music. There was one little girl, however, who was keeping perfect time. It was not that she was stronger or more capable than the other kids, in reality, she was the weakest of all. She had no motor skills whatsoever. She could not even lift her hands over her head. Thus the teacher had to stand behind her and do it all for her. The teacher knew how to do all the exercises perfectly for he had planned them. Therefore, when he did it, it was done right. Whitall observes, "She did nothing but yield herself up utterly into his hands and he did it all. The yielding was her part; the responsibility was all his . . . .The question was not of her capacity, but of his. Her utter weakness was her greatest strength."[109]

What a powerful picture that is of properly motivated, effective ministry. You don't have to be wealthy, talented, handsome, or beautiful. You do need to be surrendered, yielded to the Lord. Paul had a real physical affliction, wasn't pleasant to look at or to listen to, but God used him because he was yielded. Moses stuttered and had a criminal record, but God used him because he was yielded. Jeremiah was afraid of people but God used him to serve in a mighty way because he was yielded. John Wesley was barely 4'11" tall and had a terrible marriage, but God used him because he was yielded. D.L. Moody is said to have often murdered the English language, but what a servant he was because he was yielded. God used a shepherd boy named David, a

little boy with five loaves and two fishes, a harlot
named Rahab, an adulteress from Sychar, and a mama's
boy named John Mark. And God wants to use you. If
you yield your life to Him and to His direction the natural results will be ministry.

Jesus likened the kingdom of heaven to a pearl of
great value for which a person should be willing to give
his all. Juan Carlos Ortiz picks up on that truth in his
parable on yieldness:[110]

> "I want this pearl. How much is it?"
> "Well," the seller said, "it's very expensive."
> "But, how much?" we ask.
> "Well, a very large amount."
> "Do you think I could buy it?"
> "Oh, of course, everyone can buy it."
> "But, didn't you say it was very expensive?"
> "Yes."
> "Well, how much is it?"
> "Everything you have," says the seller.
> We make up our minds, "All right, I'll buy it," we say.
> "Well, what do you have?" he wants to know. "Let's
>   write it down."
> "Well, I have ten thousand dollars in the bank."
> "Good – ten thousand dollars. What else?"
> "That's all. That's all I have."
> "Nothing more?"
> "Well, I have a few dollars here in my pocket."
> "How much?"
> We start digging. "Well, let's see – thirty, forty, sixty,
>   eighty, a hundred, a hundred twenty dollars."
> "That's fine. What else do you have?"
> "Well, nothing. That's all."
> "Where do you live?" He's still probing.
> "In my house. Yes, I have a house."
> "The house, too, then." He writes that down.
> "You mean I have to live in my camper?"

"You have a camper? That, too. What else?"
"I'll have to sleep in my car!"
"You have a car?"
"Two of them."
"Both become mine, both cars. What else?"
"Well, you already have my money, my house, my
    camper, my cars.
What more do you want?"
"Are you alone in this world?"
"No, I have a wife and two children . . . "
"Oh, yes, your wife and children, too. What else?"
"I have nothing left! I am left alone now."
Suddenly the seller exclaims, "Oh, I almost forgot! You
    yourself, too! Everything becomes mine – wife,
    children, house, money, cars – and you too."
Then he goes on. "Now listen – I will allow you to use
    all these things for the time being. But don't forget
    that they are mine, just as you are. And whenever I
    need any of them you must give them up, because
    now I am the owner."

Have you invested in the pearl of great price? Have
you yielded your all to the Lord? Love for the Lord and
yieldness to Him naturally translates into love for and
ministry to our fellow man. John puts it this way in I
John 3:17-18:

But whoever has the world's goods, and beholds his
brother in need and closes his heart against him, how
does the love of God abide in him? Little children, let us
not love with word or with tongue, but in deed and
truth.

OUR METHOD OF MINISTRY

Let's turn to the very practical question of how we

love in deed and in truth. Ministry or service is not simply a list of things we do. It is a way of life. Therefore, there is no way to make an exhaustive list of what to do if you are a yielded servant. Instead, we need to continually be sensitive to the needs of people about us. However, let's mention some areas in which we need to be sensitive.

How do we love in deed and in truth? Be a LISTENER. In *Life Together* Dietrich Bonhoeffer identifies this as the first part of Christian service. He says, "The beginning of love for the brethren is learning to listen to them."[111] Is not this the greater part of what Paul refers to when he tells us in Galatians 6:2 to "Bear one another's burdens, and thus fulfill the law of Christ?" So many people about us each day are desperate for someone to care enough to listen to them. Most people don't need a psychiatrist, a psychologist, a counselor, or even a trained pastor. They just need someone to care enough to listen. We learned earlier that one of the most significant things we can do is to hear the confession of a brother or sister and minister to them as they struggle with accepting God's forgiveness for sins done in their past. Listening is one of the most needed ministries in today's impersonal society.

Secondly, be a HELPER. I love Richard Foster's story in this regard for it reminds me so much of myself. He was frantically trying to complete his doctoral dissertation, completely overwhelmed with busyness, when a friend called and asked him if he could take him on a few errands as he was without transportation. Cursing his luck, Foster ran out the door, but picked up Bonho-

effer's *Life Together* on the way, hoping to use his waiting time profitably. He says that he fretted and fumed
inwardly as he drove his friend from place to place.
Finally, while his friend was occupied in the supermar-
ket, Foster had the time to read, and the first words he
read were these:

> The second service that one should perform for another
> in a Christian community is that of active helpfulness.
> This means initially, simple assistance in trifling, exter-
> nal matters. There is a multitude of these things wherev-
> er people live together. Nobody is too good for the
> meanest service. One who worries about the loss of time
> that such petty, outward acts of helpfulness entail is
> usually taking the importance of his own career too
> solemnly.[112]

You see, helping is seldom convenient. If it were, it
would be of little merit. But all about us are people to be
fed. Yet when someone from the church calls us to prepare a meal for some specific need, how many of us say
we're too busy. There are people to be transported. Yet,
again, we don't want to be inconvenienced. There are
lonely people to visit. But so few ever take the time to
do it. Oh, there are people in the church like Dorcas, "a
woman abounding with deeds of kindness and charity,
which she continually did" (Acts 9:36). Among other
things she made clothes for needy people. Maybe you
could make things for people in need. Maybe you could
run errands or take people to church in your car. Maybe
you could mow the lawn of someone who is sick or
shovel the snow for a widow. Maybe you could do
some carpentry for someone who can't afford to hire it

done. What could you do to help?

You could also be a GIVER. The early church gave of their material means to the extent that no one was in need. Paul even tells us to work with our hands "in order that (we) may have something to share with him who has need" (Eph. 4:28).

Be HOSPITABLE. The Scriptures abound with admonitions to hospitality. Peter says, "Be hospitable to one another without complaint" (I Pet. 4:9). I Timothy 3:2 says that an elder or overseer is to be hospitable. In a long list of teachings on living the Christian life, Paul says in Romans 12:13 that we are to be "practicing hospitality." Hotels and restaurants are a modern-day convenience, but they will never take the place of good, old-fashioned Christian hospitality.

A Christian should also be COMPASSIONATE. I realize there is a lot of overlap in what I am saying. But I want to stress that there are people who need your compassion. James 1:27 tells us:

> This is pure and undefiled religion in the sight of our God and Father, to visit orphans and widows in their distress, and to keep oneself unstained by the world.

Are there orphans or widows who need your care and concern? In our society, it may more likely be a divorcee or the son of a single mother who has no male figure in his life. Oh, yes, there are risks and we need always to be concerned about how things appear. But Jesus many times risked being misunderstood and criticized for the sake of ministering and meeting needs.

A Christian needs also to be a RESTORER. We must

"speak the truth in love" (Eph. 4:15). That includes the confrontation of sin and stating the necessity of repentance. Again, there is great risk involved in being a restorer. You may be rejected, misunderstood, criticized and called a self-righteous hypocrite. But if your motivation is pure and it is your sincere desire to turn a person back to the Lord, it is a high and noble thing you do. It is exactly what Christ would do. James says:

> My brethren, if any among you strays from the truth, and one turns him back, let him know that he who turns a sinner from the error of his way will save his soul from death, and will cover a multitude of sins (James 5:20).

Finally, be an EVANGELIST. There is no finer ministry you can render than telling someone of Jesus and His saving power. The most significant thing you can do as a Christian is to share your faith and in so doing lead someone else to accept Jesus Christ as their Lord and Savior. That was the primary reason Christ came to this earth, "to seek and to save that which was lost" (Luke 11:10). How can you love your lost friends and neighbors in deed and in truth? You have not really shown love until you have tried to show them Jesus. Hear the words of Paul:

> Therefore, we are ambassadors for Christ, as though God were entreating through us; we beg you on behalf of Christ, be reconciled to God. He made Him who knew no sin to be sin on our behalf, that we might become the righteousness of God in Him (II Cor. 5:20-21).

My preacher friend said that we deepen spiritually as we reach out evangelistically. I believe he is right. But it should also be true that we reach out evangelistically as we deepen spiritually. My brother wrote, "It is evangelism more than anything else that has given the Spirit a chance to grow His fruit in me." I covet that experience for you as well; not only for your sake, but for the sake of the lost you can reach. Another preacher friend wrote, "Whenever I get a little low spiritually, I go and talk to someone who needs the Lord. This always strengthens my personal faith." May you also grow through ministry, especially the ministry of bringing others to Christ.

CONCLUSION

Most Christians struggle with the issue of balance in their Christian life. I know I do. We begin to emphasize our devotional life and soon we're so busy practicing the devotional disciplines that we're no longer involved in ministry. Or we emphasize ministry to the extent that we're left hollow and empty in the inner man, and our work for the Lord is done in the power of the flesh. I really believe the latter has been true of the modern day church far more often than the former. This book has been an attempt to push us toward a greater emphasis on the spiritual development of the inner man that we might in turn be involved in Spirit-motivated, Spirit-empowered ministry. May none of us be deceived of Satan into thinking the Christian life is to be spiritual depth OR ministry. It is to be both. To me the reading, "I

Stand By the Door" by Samuel Moor Shoemaker speaks of the balance I seek in my life and which I desire for each one of you.

> I stand by the door.
> I neither go too far in, nor stay too far out,
> The door is the most important door in the world –
> It is the door through which men walk when they find
>   God.
> There's no use my going way inside, and staying there,
> When so many are still outside and they, as much as I,
> Crave to know where the door is.
> And all that so many ever find
> Is only the wall where a door ought to be.
> They creep along the wall like blind men,
> With outstretched, groping hands.
> Feeling for a door, knowing there must be a door,
> Yet they never find it . . . .
> So I stand by the door.
>   The most tremendous thing in the world
> Is for men to find that door – the door to God.
> The most important thing any man can do
> Is to take hold of one of those blind, groping hands,
> And put it on the latch – the latch that only clicks
> And opens to the man's own touch.
> Men die outside that door, as starving beggars die
> On cold nights in cruel cities in the dead of winter –
> Die for want of what is within their grasp.
> They live, on the other side of it – live because they have
>   not found it,
> Nothing else matters compared to helping them find it,
> And open it, and walk in, and find him . . . .
> So I stand by the door.
> Go in, great saints, go all the way in –
> Go way down into the cavernous cellars,
> And way up into the spacious attics –
> It is a vast, roomy house, this house where God is
> Go into the deepest of hidden casements,
> Of withdrawal, of silence, of sainthood.

Some must inhabit those inner rooms,
And know the depth and heights of God,
And call outside to the rest of us how wonderful it is.
Sometimes I take a deeper look in,
Sometimes venture in a little farther;
But my place seems closer to the opening . . . .
So I stand by the door.
  There is another reason why I stand there.
Some people get part way in and become afraid
Lest God and the zeal of his house devour them;
For God is so very great, and asks all of us.
And these people feel a cosmic claustrophobia,
And want to get out. `Let me out!' they cry.
And the people way inside only terrify them more.
Somebody must be by the door to tell them that they are
    spoiled
For the old life, they have seen too much:
Once taste God, and nothing but God will do any more.
Somebody must be watching for the frightened
Who seek to sneak out just where they came in,
To tell them how much better it is inside.
  The people too far in do not see how near these are
To leaving – preoccupied with the wonder of it all.
Somebody must watch for those who have entered the
    door,
But would like to run away. So for them, too,
I stand by the door.
I admire the people who go way in.
But I wish they would not forget how it was
Before they got in. Then they would be able to help
The people who have not yet even found the door,
Or the people who want to run away again from God.
You can go in too deeply, and stay in too long,
And forget the people outside the door.
As for me, I shall take my old accustomed place,
Near enough to God to hear him, and know he is there,
But not so far from men as not to hear them,
And remember they are there, too.
Where? Outside the door –
Thousands of them, millions of them.

But – more important for me –
One of them, two of them, ten of them,
Whose hands I am intended to put on the latch.
So I shall stand by the door and wait
   for those who seek it.
"I had rather be a door-keeper . . . "
So I stand by the door.[113]

THOUGHT QUESTIONS:

1. What do you consider to be the primary benefit of the pursuit of spiritual growth?

2. Why might some people resist an emphasis on Christian disciplines for spiritual growth?

3. What do you consider to be the primary danger of an emphasis on spiritual growth?

4. What was the primary lesson Jesus was trying to get across when He washed the feet of the disciples?

5. How is what Christ did at the Last Supper representative of His whole life?

6. In thinking about your own ministry in the church or your service to others, what do you believe is your primary motivation?

7. Do you recognize any of the improper motivations mentioned in this chapter as being present in your life?

8. If yieldedness should naturally result in service, what are some of the reasons why so many professing Christians are very little involved in ministry?

9. Do you feel you have yielded all to the Lord? What are you holding back? Be honest with yourself and with Him.

10. Have you been convicted of the need to be involved in a particular area of ministry? Which one? What are you going to do about it?

ASSIGNMENTS:

Identify the way(s) you *are* ministering through the church.

Identify the way(s) in which you *will* minister through the church.

Identify the following:

Someone for whom you can be a listener:

Some way in which you can be a helper:

Some need for which you can be a giver:

Someone to whom and some way in which you can be hospitable:

Someone toward whom you should be compassionate:

Someone for whom you can be a restorer:

Someone to whom you can be a evangelist:

Put into action a plan by which you can minister in the ways you've identified.

SCRIPTURE REFERENCES:

John 4:34	Mark 9:35	I Peter 4:9
Luke 19:10	Matthew 25:31-46	I Timothy 3:2
Mark 10:43-45	I John 3:17-18	Romans 12:13
Luke 22:25-27	Matthew 13:44	James 1:27
John 13:3-17	Galatians 6:2	Ephesians 4:15
Philippians 2:5-11	Acts 9:36	James 5:20
Isaiah 14:12-14	Ephesians 4:28	I Cor. 5:20-21

RECOMMENDED READING:

Improving Your Serve by Charles Swindoll
Christ's Call To Discipleship by James Montgomery
  Boice

QUOTABLE QUOTES:

"Learn the lesson that, if you are to do the work of a prophet, what you need is not a scepter but a hoe."
–Bernard of Clairvaux

"Make us worthy, Lord, to serve our fellow men throughout the world who live and die in poverty and hunger. Give them, through our hands, this day their daily bread, and by our understanding love give Peace and Joy. Lord, make me a channel of thy peace, that where there is hatred I may bring love; that where there is wrong, I may bring the spirit of forgiveness; that where there is discord, I may bring harmony; that where there is error, I may bring truth; that where there is doubt, I may bring faith; that where there is despair, I may bring hope; that where there are shadows, I may bring light; that where there is sadness, I may bring joy.

Lord, grant that I may seek rather to comfort than to be comforted; to understand than to be understood; to love than to be loved; for it is by forgetting self that one finds; it is by dying that one awakens to eternal life. Amen."

–From SOMETHING BEAUTIFUL FOR GOD
by Malcolm Muggeridge

APPENDIX

CHRISTIAN DISCIPLINES SURVEY
INDIANAPOLIS AREA MINISTERS

AGE: ( )under 25 ( )26-35 ( )36-45 ( )46-55 ( )over 55

1. Do you have a consistent, daily devotional time?
( ) yes ( ) no

2. How much time per day (on the average) do you spend in prayer?
( ) none
( ) 1 minute or less
( ) 1-5 minutes
( ) 5-15 minutes
( ) 15-30 minutes
( ) 30-60 minutes
( ) more than an hour

3. Do you maintain a prayer list?
( ) yes ( ) no

4. Do you keep a spiritual journal?
( ) yes ( ) no

5. Have you ever kept a spiritual journal?
( ) yes ( ) no

6. How often have you fasted for spiritual reasons?
( ) never
( ) once

( ) several times
( ) often
( ) regularly

7. How often do you read the Scriptures for your own personal, spiritual growth?
( ) daily
( ) two or three times a week
( ) weekly
( ) occasionally
( ) rarely

8. How many books have you read in the past twelve months to aid you in your spiritual growth?
( ) none
( ) one
( ) two to five
( ) six to ten
( ) ten to twenty
( ) more than twenty

9. Is there a person(s) to whom you make yourself spiritually accountable?
( ) yes ( ) no

10. Are you presently a part of a discipleship group of any kind?
( ) yes ( ) no

11. In the past twelve months, have you attended a retreat, conference, or seminar for your own personal spiritual growth?
( ) yes ( ) no

12. On a scale of 0-10 (10 being very satisfied) how satisfied are you with your inward spiritual life?
0   1   2   3   4   5   6   7   8   9   10

Comments:

CHRISTIAN DISCIPLINES SURVEY
INDIANAPOLIS AREA MINISTERS RESULTS

AGE: 3%—under 25   45%—26-35   27%—36-45
12%—46-55 13%—over 55

1. Do you have a consistent, daily devotional time?
    61% – yes   39% – no

2. How much time per day (on the average) do you spend in prayer?
    0%   – none
    1.5%   – 1 minute or less
    12%   – 1-5 minutes
    36%   – 5-15 minutes
    34%   – 15-30 minutes
    12%   – 30-60 minutes
    4.5%   – more than an hour

3. Do you maintain a prayer list?
    76% – yes   24% – no

4. Do you keep a spiritual journal?
    18% – yes   82% – no

5. Have you ever kept a spiritual journal?
    40% – yes   60% – no

6. How often have you fasted for spiritual reasons?
    9%   – never
    15%   – once
    59%   – several times
    9%   – often
    8%   – regularly

7. How often do you read the Scriptures for your own personal, spiritual growth?

        55%   – daily
        27%   – two or three times a week
        10.5% – weekly
        6%   – occasionally
        1.5%   – rarely

8. How many books have you read in the past twelve months to aid you in your spiritual growth?

        2%   – none
        3%   – one
        46%   – two to five
        32%   – six to ten
        12%   – ten to twenty
        5%   – more than twenty

9. Is there a person(s) to whom you make yourself spiritually accountable?

        48% – yes   52% – no

10. Are you presently a part of a discipleship group of any kind?

        45% – yes   55% – no

11. In the past twelve months, have you attended a retreat, conference, or seminar for your own personal spiritual growth?

        77% – yes   23% – no

12. On a scale of 0-10 (10 being very satisfied) how satisfied are you with your inward spiritual life?

0	1	2	3	4	5	6	7	8	9	10
0%	3%	6%	13%	5%	25%	17%	16%	11%	2%	2%

CHRISTIAN DISCIPLINES SURVEY

Are you a Christian? ( )yes ( )no

Are you a Kingsway member? ( )yes ( )no

AGE: ( )12 or under ( )13-19 ( )20-30 ( )31-40 ( )41-50
( )51-65 ( )over 65

1. Do you have a consistent, daily devotional time?
( ) yes ( ) no

2. How much time per day (on the average) do you
spend in prayer?
( ) none
( ) 1 minute or less
( ) 1-5 minutes
( ) 5-15 minutes
( ) 15-30 minutes
( ) 30-60 minutes
( ) more than an hour

3. Do you maintain a prayer list?
( ) yes ( ) no

4. Do you keep a spiritual journal?
( ) yes ( ) no

5. Have you ever kept a spiritual journal?
( ) yes ( ) no

6. How often have you fasted for spiritual reasons?

( ) never
( ) once
( ) several times

( ) regularly

7. How often do you read the Bible?
    ( ) daily
    ( ) two or three times a week
    ( ) weekly
    ( ) occasionally
    ( ) rarely

8. How many books have you read in the past year to aid you in your spiritual growth?
    ( ) none
    ( ) one
    ( ) two to five
    ( ) six to ten
    ( ) more than ten

9. Is there a person(s) to whom you make yourself spiritually accountable?
    ( ) Yes ( ) No

10. Are you presently a part of a discipleship group of any kind?
    ( ) yes ( ) no

11. In the past twelve months, have you attended a retreat, conference, or seminar for your own personal, spiritual growth?
    ( ) yes ( ) no

12. On a scale of 0-10 (10 being very satisfied) how satisfied are you with your inward spiritual life?
0 1 2 3 4 5 6 7 8 9 10
Comments:

CHRISTIAN DISCIPLINES SURVEY – RESULTS

Are you a Christian? 97% – yes 3% – no

Are you a Kingsway member? 89% – yes 11% – no

Age: 5.3%—12 or under 14.5%—13-19 15.6%—20-30
27.4%—31-40 20.9%—41-50 12%—51-65 4.2%—over 65

1. Do you have a consistent, daily devotional time?
     36% – yes   64% – no

2. How much time per day (on the average) do you
spend in prayer?
     5%   – none
     11.9%   – 1 minute or less
     37.3%   – 1-5 minutes
     30.9%   – 5-15 minutes
     10.2%   – 15-30 minutes
     3.1%   – 30-60 minutes
     1.3%   – more than an hour

3. Do you maintain a prayer list?
     30% – yes   70% – no

4. Do you keep a spiritual journal?
     6.3% – yes   93.7% – no

5. Have you ever kept a spiritual journal?
     20.2% – yes   79.8% – no

6. How often have you fasted for spiritual reasons?
     53%   – never
     22%   – once
     24%   – several times

1%   – regularly

7. How often do you read the Bible?
    22.4%   – daily
    23.6%   – two or three times a week
    16.3%   – weekly
    24.3%   – occasionally
    13.4%   – rarely

8. How many books have you read in the past year to aid you in your spiritual growth?
    41%   – none
    22%   – one
    28.4%   – two to five
    5.5%   – six to ten
    2.9%   – more than ten

9. Is there a person to whom you make yourself spiritually accountable?
    40.8% – yes   59.2% – no

10. Are you presently part of a discipleship group of any kind?
    24.4% – yes   75.6% – no

11. In the past 12 months, have you attended a retreat, conference, or seminar for your own personal spiritual growth?
    35.4% – yes   64.6% – no

12. On a scale of 0-10 (10 being very satisfied), how satisfied are you with your inward spiritual life?

0	1	2	3	4	5	6	7	8	9	10
2.5%	7%	6.4%	15%	16.4%	24%	9.5%	9%	7.6%	1.2%	1.2%

CHRISTIAN DISCIPLINES SURVEY – PART II

Are you a Christian? ( )yes ( )no
Are you a Kingsway member? ( )yes ( )no
Have you been a regular attendee during this series?
( )yes ( )no

AGE: ( )12 or under ( )13-19 ( )20-30 ( )31-40 ( )41-50
( )51-65 ( )over 65

1. Do you have a consistent, daily devotional time?
( ) yes ( ) no

Did you begin during this series? ( )yes ( )no

2. How much time per day (on the average) do you spend in prayer?

( ) none
( ) 1 minute or less
( ) 1-5 minutes
( ) 5-15 minutes
( ) 15-30 minutes
( ) 30-60 minutes
( ) more than an hour

Does this represent an increase during this series?
( )yes ( )no

3. Do you maintain a prayer list? ( ) yes ( ) no
Did you begin during this series? ( )yes ( ) no

4. Do you keep a spiritual journal? ( ) yes ( ) no
Did you begin during this series? ( )yes ( )no

5. How often have you fasted for spiritual reasons?
( ) never
( ) once
( ) several times
( ) regularly

Have you started during this series? ( )yes ( )no

6. How often do you read the Bible?
( ) daily
( ) two or three times a week
( ) weekly
( ) occasionally
( ) rarely

Has the frequency increased during this series?
( )yes ( )no

7. How many books do you anticipate reading for your spiritual growth during this coming year?
( ) none
( ) one
( ) two to five
( ) six to ten
( ) more than ten

8. Please indicate the disciplines in which you have made specific progress as a result of this series:
( ) Prayer
( ) Confession
( ) Journaling
( ) Reading
( ) Bible Study
( ) Meditation

( ) Devotional Life
( ) Fasting
( ) Personal Worship
( ) Ministry

Please UNDERLINE the discipline which was the subject of the most helpful message to you.

9. Do you feel you have grown spiritually through this series?

     ( ) yes ( ) no

10. How often did you make use of the worksheets?

     ( ) never
     ( ) occasionally
     ( ) regularly
     ( ) every week

Comments:

CHRISTIAN DISCIPLINES
SURVEY – PART II RESULTS

Are you a Christian? 97.6% – yes 2.4% – no
Are you a Kingsway member?
    88.3% – yes 11.7% – no
Have you been a regular attendee during this series?
    85.5% – yes 4.5% – no

AGE: 3.7%—12 or under 3.3%—13-19 16.5%—20-30
32.4%—31-40 16.1%—41-50 14.2%—51-65 3.8%—over
65

1. Do you have a consistent, daily devotional time?
    54.5% – yes   45.5% – no

Did you begin during this series?
    27.8% – yes   72.2% – no

2. How much time per day (on the average) do you
spend in prayer?

3%	– none
4.6%	– 1 minute or less
29.8%	– 1-5 minutes
37.3%	– 5-15 minutes
19%	– 15-30 minutes
4.4%	– 30-60 minutes
1.6%	– more than an hour

Does this represent an increase during this series?
    51% – yes   49% – no

3. Do you maintain a prayer list?
    42% – yes 58% – no

Did you begin during this series?
    18.5% – yes 81.5% – no

4. Do you keep a spiritual journal?
    19% – yes 81% – no

Did you begin during this series?
    11.4% – yes 88.6% – no

5. How often have you fasted for spiritual reasons?
    50.7%   – never
    16.9%   – once
    30.6%   – several times
    1.7%   – regularly

Have you started during this series?
    10% – yes 90% – no

6. How often do you read the Bible?
    35.4%   – daily
    31.3%   – two or three times a week
    12.3%   – weekly
    14.7%   – occasionally
    6.3%   – rarely

Has the frequency increased during this series?
    42% – yes 58% – no

7. How many books do you anticipate reading for your spiritual growth during this coming year?
    19.5%   – none
    19.3%   – one

48.4%   – two to five
6.7%   – six to ten
6.1%   – more than ten

8. Please indicate the disciplines in which you have made specific progress as a result of this series: (figures represent the percentage of the total of all disciplines indicated)

20.8%   – Prayer
13.8%   – Bible Study
13.4%   – Personal Worship
10.7%   – Meditation
10.4%   – Reading
9.4%   – Confession
8.3%   – Devotional Life
5.7%   – Ministry
4.5%   – Journaling
3%   – Fasting

Please UNDERLINE the discipline which was the subject of the most helpful message to you.

13.8%   – Personal Worship
13.3%   – Prayer
13.3%   – Bible Study
12.5%   – Devotional Life
12.1%   – Meditation
10.8%   – Ministry
7.1%   – Journaling
6.7%   – Confession
5.4%   – Reading
.5%   – Fasting

9. Do you feel you have grown spiritually through

this series?
>   89.4% – yes 10.6% – no

10. How often did you make use of the worksheets?
>   24.8%   – never
>   51.3%   – occasionally
>   .7%   – regularly
>   6.9%   – every week

SURVEY I   SURVEY II

	SURVEY I	SURVEY II
Participants who have a consistent daily devotional time:	36%	54.5%
Amount of time per day spent in prayer:		
None	5%	3%
1 minute or less	11.9%	4.6%
1-5 minutes	37.3%	29.8%
5-15 minutes	30.9%	37.3%
15-30 minutes	10.2%	19%
30-60 minutes	3.1%	4.4%
more than an hour	1.3%	1.6%
Participants maintaining a prayer list:	30%	42%
Participants keeping a spiritual journal:	6.3%	19%
Frequency of the practice of fasting:		
never	53%	50.7%
once	22%	16.9%
several times	24%	30.6%

regularly	1%	1.7%
Frequency of Bible reading:		
daily	22.4%	35.4%
2-3 times a week	23.6%	31.3%
weekly	16.3%	12.3%
occasionally	24.3%	14.7%
rarely	13.4%	6.3%

Books read (I) and books anticipated read (II):

none	41%	19.5%
1	22%	19.3%
2-5	28.4%	48.4%
6-10	5.5%	6.7%
more than 10	2.9%	6.1%

$\mathcal{N}otes$

Chapter 1
Born To Grow

1. John MacMillan, *The Authority Of The Believer*, (Harrisburg, PA: Christian Publications, 1980), pp. 5-6.

2. Reuben Job and Norman Shawchuck, *A Guide To Prayer For Ministers & Other Servants*, (Nashville: Upper Room, 1983), p. 34.

3. Calvin Miller, *The Table of Inwardness*, (Downers Grove: Inter-Varsity, 1984) p. 13.

4. Miller, p. 17.

5. Gordon MacDonald, *Restoring Your Spiritual Passion*, (Nashville: Oliver Nelson, 1986).

6. Ken Idleman, personal correspondence, Joplin, MO, Dec. 16, 1987.

7. Bob Yawberg, personal correspondence, Ft. Wayne, IN, Dec. 17, 1987.

8. Job, p. 283.

9. Job, p. 226.

10. Richard Foster, *Celebration Of Discipline*, (San Francisco: Harper & Row, 1978), pp. 8-9.

11. L.D. Campbell, personal correspondence, Florence, KY, Dec. 30, 1987.

12. Larnelle Harris, *I Miss My Time With You*, (Nashville: Lifesong Music, 1986).

Chapter 2
Growing Through Prayer

13. Larry Bryant, *Shopping List*, (Nashville: Meadowgreen Music Co., 1984).

14. Jack Taylor, *Prayer: Life's Limitless Reach*, (Nashville: Broadman, 1977), p. 12.

15. W.F. Lown, personal correspondence, Joplin, MO, Dec. 31, 1987.

16. Andrea Sterk and Peter Scazzero, *Christian Disciplines*, (Downers Grove: InterVarsity, 1985), p. 13.

17. Taylor, p. 34.

18. E.M. Bounds, *Power Through Prayer*, (Grand Rapids: Zondervan, 1961), p. 52.

19. Dick Eastman, *No Easy Road*, (Grand Rapids: Baker, 1971), p. 19.

20. Eastman, pp. 101-102.

21. Curtis Mitchell, *Praying Jesus' Way*, (Old Tappan, NJ: Revell, 1977), p. 142.

Chapter 3
Growing Through Confession

22. Warren Myers, *How To Be Effective In Prayer*, (Colorado Springs: NavPress, 1983), p. 16.

23. Charles Keyson, *Come Clean!*, (Wheaton: Victor, 1976), p. 28.

24. J. Oswald Sanders, *Prayer Power Unlimited*, (Chicago: Moody, 1977), p. 17.

25. Source unknown.

26. Myers, p. 17.

27. Keyson, pp. 37-38.

28. Richard Foster, *Celebration Of Discipline*, (San Francisco: Harper & Row, 1978), p. 129.

29. Walter Luthi and Edward Thurneysen, *Preaching, Confession, The Lord's Supper*, (Richmond, VA: John Knox, 1957), p. 55.

30. Luthi, pp. 61-62.

31. Foster, p. 137.

Chapter 4
Growing Through Reading And Writing

32. Richard Foster, *Celebration Of Discipline*, (San Francisco: Harper & Row, 1978), p. 1.

33. Foster, p. 54.

34. Ronald Klug, *How To Keep A Spiritual Journal*, (Nashville: Nelson, 1982), p. 11.

35. Klug, p. 9.

36. Klug, pp. 17-26.

37. Bob and Michael Benson, *Disciplines For The Inner Life*, (Waco, TX: Word, 1985), p. 99.

38. Benson, p. 98.

39. Benson, p. 101.

40. David and Karen Mains, *The Godhunt*, (Chicago: David C. Cook, 1984).

41. John Wesley, *The Journal Of John Wesley*, (Chicago: Moody, n.d.), p. 33.

42. Wesley, pp. 166-167.

43. Wesley, p. 241.

44. Wesley, p. 379.
45. Douglas Rumford, "Keeping a Personal Journal." *Leadership 3* (Winter 1982), p. 56.
46. Ibid.

Chapter 5
Growing Through Bible Study

47. Henry H. Halley, *Bible Handbook*, (Grand Rapids: Zondervan, 1962), p. 805.
48. Homer Hathaway, "Who Reads the Bible Today?" *Christian Standard*, 4 October, 1970, pp. 9-10.
49. Andrew Murray, *The Inner Life*, (Grand Rapids: Zondervan, 1980), pp. 67ff.
50. Irving Jensen, *How To Profit From Bible Reading*, (Chicago: Moody, 1985), pp. 12-13.
51. Knofel Staton, personal correspondence, Fullerton, Ca., Dec. 21, 1987.
52. Bob and Michael Benson, *Disciplines For The Inner Life*, (Waco, TX: Word, 1985), p. 91.
53. *The Navigator Bible Studies Handbook*, (Colorado Springs: NavPress, 1974), p. 23.
54. Clay Cooper, "Four Reasons Why We Need the Bible." *Christian Standard*, 15 October, 1966, p. 7.
55. Cooper, p. 8.
56. John White, *Bible Study*, p. 30.
57. Oswald J. Smith, *How To Read the Bible*, a tract printed by The People's Church of Willowdale, Ontario, Canada.

Chapter 6
Growing Through Meditation

58. Charles Hummel, *Tyranny Of The Urgent*, (Downers Grove: InterVarsity, 1967), p. 3
59. Jean Fleming, *Between Walden & The Whirlwind*, (Colorado Springs: NavPress, 1985), p. 47.
60. Bob and Michael Benson, *Disciplines For The Inner Life*, (Waco, TX: Word, 1985), p. 47.
61. Benson, p. 49.
62. Henri Nouwen, *Making All Things New*, (San Francisco: Harper & Row, 1981), p. 69.
63. Benson, p. 37.
64. Benson, p. 48.
65. Richard Foster, *Meditative Power*, (Downers Grove: InterVarsity, 1983), pp. 21-22.

66. Lynne Hybels, *The Joy Of Personal Worship*, (Wheaton: Victor Books, 1984), p. 116.

67. Nouwen, p. 77.

68. Irving Jensen, *How To Profit From Bible Reading*, (Chicago: Moody, 1985), pp. 48-52.

69. Jim Downing, *Meditation*, (Colorado Springs: NavPress, 1976), p. 27.

70. Kenneth Leech, *Soul Friend*, (San Francisco: Harper & Row, 1977), p. 178.

71. Downing, p. 36.

72. Richard Foster, *Celebration Of Discipline* (San Francisco: Harper & Row, 1978), p. 17.

73. William Barclay, *Daily Celebration*, Vol. 2, (Waco, TX: Word, 1973), p. 165.

74. E. Stanley Jones, *A Song Of Assent*, (Nashville: Abingdon, 1968), p. 29.

Chapter 7
Growing Through The Devotional Life

75. Terry Muck, "Ten Questions About the Devotional Life." *Leadership 3* (Winter 1982); p. 30.

76. Robert Foster, *Seven Minutes With God*, (Colorado Springs: NavPress, n.d.), p. 2.

77. Maxie Dunham, *The Workbook On Spiritual Disciplines*, (Nashville: Upper Room, 1984), p. 7.

78. Dunham, p. 8.

79. Frank Houghton, *Quiet Time*, (Downers Grove: InterVarsity, 1976), p. 9.

80. A.J. Conyers, *How To Read The Bible*, (Downers Grove: InterVarsity, 1986), p. 153.

81. Jack Taylor, *Prayer: Life's Limitless Reach*, (Nashville: Broadman, 1977), p. 103.

82. Houghton, pp. 25-30.

Chapter 8
Growing Through Fasting

83. Don DeWelt, *Prayer & Fasting*, (Joplin, MO: Ozark Bible College, n.d.).

84. Arthur Wallis, *God's Chosen Fast*, (Fort Washington, PA: Christian Literature Crusade, p. 23.

85. Wallis, p. 136.

86. Richard Foster, "Fasting: Twentieth Century Style," *Theological Students Fellowship Bulletin*, Nov.-Dec. 1983), p. 15.

87. Bob and Michael Benson, *Disciplines Of The Inner Life*, (Waco, TX: Word, 1985), p. 112.

88. J. Oswald Sanders, *Prayer Power Unlimited*, (Chicago: Moody, 1977), p. 67.

89. Sanders, p. 68.

90. Wallis, p. 32.

91. Foster, p. 16.

92. Ibid.

93. Wallis, p. 108.

Chapter 9
Growing Through Personal Worship

94. J. Oswald Sanders, *Prayer Power Unlimited*, (Chicago: Moody, 1977), p. 21.

95. John MacArthur, *The Ultimate Priority*, (Chicago: Moody, 1983), p. 1.

96. Lynne Hybels, *The Joy Of Personal Worship*, (Wheaton: Victor Books, 1984), p. 53.

97. Brother Lawrence, *The Practice Of The Presence Of God*, (Old Tappan, NJ: Spire, 1958), p. 32.

98. Richard Foster, *Celebration Of Discipline*, (San Francisco: Harper & Row, 1978), p. 138.

99. Warren and Ruth Myers, *Praise: A Door To God's Presence*, (Colorado Springs: NavPress, 1987), p. 34.

100. Foster, p. 148.

101. Hybels, p. 133.

102. Sanders, p. 20.

103. Sanders, p. 21.

Chapter 10
Growing Through Ministry

104. Personal Correspondence, December 22, 1987.

105. James Montgomery Boice, *Christ's Call To Discipleship*, (Chicago: Moody, 1986), p. 62.

106. Boice, p. 61.

107. Richard Foster, *Celebration Of Discipline*, (San Francisco: Harper & Row, 1978), pp. 112-113.

108. Charles Swindoll, *Improving Your Serve*, (Waco: Word, 1981), pp. 43-44.

109. Hannah Whitall Smith, *The Christian's Secret Of A Happy Life*, (Old Tappan, NJ: Revell, 1970), p. 135.

110. Maxie Dunham, *The Workbook On Spiritual Disciplines*, (Nashville: Upper Room, 1984), pp. 137-138.

111. Boice, p. 62.

112. Foster, pp. 117-118.

113. Reuben Job and Norman Shawchuck, pp. 305-306.

Spiritual Disciplines Resource List

Adeney, Carol. ed. *This Morning With God*. Downers Grove: InterVarsity, 1978.

Allison, Joseph O. *The Devotional Resource Guide*. Nashville: Nelson, 1986.

Anderson, Andy. *Fasting Changed My Life*. Nashville: Broadman, n.d.

Andrews, C.F. *Christ In The Silence*. New York: Abingdon, 1933.

Augsburger, Myron. *Called To Maturity*. Scottsdale, PA: Herald Press, 1960.

Augustine. *Confessions*. Translated by Edward Pusey. New York: Macmillan, 1961.

Barclay, William. *Daily Celebration, vol.* 2. Waco, TX: Word, 1973.

Bainton, Roland H. *Here I Stand*. Nashville: Abingdon, 1950.

Beall, James Lee. *The Adventure of Fasting*. Old Tappan, NJ: Revell, 1974.

Belden, Albert. *The Practice of Prayer*. New York: Harper & Brothers, n.d.

Bennett, Arthur, ed. *Valley of Vision*. Edinburgh: Banner of Truth, 1975.

Benson, Bob, and Michael W. Benson. *Disciplines For The Inner Life*. Waco, TX: Word, 1985.

Bernardin, Joseph. *The Ministry of Service*. Collegeville, MN: Liturgical Press, 1985.

Bewes, Richard. *Talking About Prayer*. Downers Grove: InterVarsity, 1979.

Bisagno, John. *The Power of Positive Praying*. Grand Rapids: Zondervan, 1965.

Blanchard, Charles A. *Getting Things From God*. Chicago: Bible Institute Colportage Assoc., 1915.

Bloom, Anthony. *Beginning To Pray*. New York: Paulist, 1970.

_____. *Courage To Pray*. New York: Paulist, 1973.

_____. *God & Man*. New York: Paulist, 1971.

_____. *Living Prayer*. London: Libra, 1966.

Boice, James Montgomery. *Christ's Call to Discipleship*. Chicago: Moody, 1986.

Bonhoeffer, Dietrich. *The Cost of Discipleship*. New York: Macmillan, 1949.

_____. *Life Together*. New York: Harper & Row, 1954.

_____. *The Martyred Christian*. Joan Winmill Brown, ed. New York: Macmillan, 1983.

_____. *Meditating On The Word*. Cambridge, MA: Cowley, 1986.

Bounds, Edward M. *The Essentials of Prayer*. New York: Revell, 1925.

_____. *The Necessity Of Prayer*. New York: Revell, 1925.

_____. *The Possibilities Of Prayer*. Grand Rapids: Baker, 1979.

_____. *Power Through Prayer*. Grand Rapids: Zondervan, 1961.

_____. *Prayer And The Praying Man*. New York: Doran, 1921.

_____. *Purpose In Prayer*. Chicago: Moody, 1980.

_____ . *The Reality Of Prayer*. Chicago: Moody, 1980.

_____ . *A Treasury Of Prayer*. Minneapolis: Bethany Fellowship, 1961.

_____ . *The Weapon Of Prayer*. New York: Revell, 1931.

Bowman, George William III. *The Dynamics Of Confession*. Richmond, VA: John Knox, n.d.

Brainerd, David. *The Life Of David Brainerd*. Grand Rapids: Baker, 1978.

Bridges, Jerry. *The Pursuit Of Godliness*. Colorado Springs: NavPress, n.d.

_____ . *The Pursuit of Holiness*. Colorado Springs: NavPress, 1978.

Briscoe, D. Stuart. *Getting Into God*. Grand Rapids: Zondervan, 1975.

Bryant, Larry. *Shopping List*. Nashville: Meadowgreen Music, 1984.

Bubeck, Mark I. *The Adversary*. Chicago: Moody, 1984.

Bunyan, John. *The Pilgrim's Progress*. Old Tappan, NJ: Revell, 1965.

Cargas, Harry J., and Roger Radley. *Keeping A Spiritual Journal*. Garden City, NJ: Doubleday, 1981.

Casteel, John L. *Rediscovering Prayer*. New York: Association Press, 1955.

Chambers, Oswald. *My Utmost For His Highest*. New York: Dodd, Mead, & Co., n.d.

Clark, Kelly James. *Quiet Times For Christian Growth*. Downers Grove: InterVarsity, 1979.

Claydon, Graham. *Time With God*. Grand Rapids: Zondervan, 1979.

Clowney, Edmund P. *Christian Meditation*. Nutley, NJ: Craig Press, 1979.

Colson, Charles W. *Born Again*. Falls Church, VA: Conservative Press, 1976.

Conyers, A.J. *How To Read The Bible*. Downers Grove: InterVarsity, 1986.

Conwell, Russell N. *Acres Of Diamonds*. Old Tappan, NJ: Revell, 1975.

Cooper, Clay. *"Four Reasons Why We Need The Bible."* Christian Standard, 15 October 1966, 7-8.

Cowman, Mrs. Charles E. *Streams In The Desert*. Grand Rapids: Zondervan, 1965.

de Foucauld, Charles. *Meditations Of A Hermit*. London: Burns & Oates, n.d.

de Sales, Francis. *Introduction To A Devout Life*. New York: World Publishing, 1952.

DeWelt, Don. *Prayer and Fasting*. Joplin, MO: Ozark Bible College, n.d. Typewritten.

_____. *Prayer Time, A Guide For Personal Worship*. Joplin, MO: College Press, 1982.

Downing, Jim. *Meditation*. Colorado Springs: NavPress, 1976.

Dunham, Maxie. *The Workbook On Spiritual Disciplines*. Nashville: Upper Room, 1984.

Eastman, Dick. *The Hour That Changes The World*. Grand Rapids: Baker, 1978.

_____. *No Easy Road*. Grand Rapids: Baker, 1971.

Edwards, Jonathan. *Life And Diary of David Brainerd*. New Haven, Conn.: Yale University Press, 1984.

Elliff, Thomas, D. *Praying For Others*. Nashville: Broadman, 1979.

Elliott, Elizabeth. *Through Gates Of Splendor*. New York: Harper & Row, 1958.

Falwell, Jerry. *Fasting*. Wheaton: Tyndale House, 1981.

Fee, Gordon, and Douglas Stuart. *How To Read The Bible For All It's Worth*. Grand Rapids: Zondervan, 1982.

Fenhagen, James C. *More Than Wanderers*. New York: Seabury, 1978.

Ferré, Nels. *Strengthening The Spiritual Life*. New York: Harper & Brothers, 1951.

Finley, James. *The Awakening Call*. Notre Dame, Ind.: Ave Maria Press, n.d.

Fleming, Jean. *Between Walden And The Whirlwind*. Colorado Springs: NavPress, n.d.

Fosdick, Harry Emerson. *The Meaning Of Prayer*. Nashville: Abingdon, 1949.

Foster, Lewis. *Selecting A Translation Of The Bible*. Cincinnati: Standard, 1983.

Foster, Richard J. *Celebration Of Discipline*. San Francisco: Harper & Row, 1978.

_____ . "Fasting: Twentieth Century Style." *Theological Students Fellowship Bulletin* (November-December 1983): 14-16.

_____ . *Prayer: Finding the Heart's True Home*. San Francisco: Harper, 1992.

_____ . *Meditative Prayer*. Downers Grove: InterVarsity, 1983.

Foster, Richard J., and Henri Nouwen. "Hearing God's Voice and . . . : Interview with Richard J. Foster and Henri Nouwen," interview by Terry Muck. Harold Myra, and Roy Coffman, *Leadership 3* (Winter 1982): 16-29.

Foster, Robert D. *Seven Minutes With God*. Colorado Springs: NavPress, n.d.

God's Power Through Prayer. Houston: Countryman Pub., n.d.

Gordon, S.D. *Quiet Talks On How To Pray*. New York: Revell, 1929.

_____ . *Quiet Talks On Service*. New York: Revell, 1906.

Gritter, George. *The Quest For Holiness*. Grand Rapids: Eerdmans, 1955.

Growing Strong in God's Family. Colorado Springs: NavPress, 1987.

Gunsaulus, Frank W. *The Minister and Spiritual Life*. New York: Revell, 1911.

Hanson, Bradley. *The Call of Silence*. Minneapolis: Augsburg, 1980.

Halley, Henry H. *Bible Handbook*. Grand Rapids: Zondervan, 1962.

Halverson, Richard C. *No Greater Power*. Portland, OR: Multnomah, 1986.

Hathaway, Homer, "Who Reads the Bible Today?" *Christian Standard*. 4 October 1970, 9-10.

Henderson, Lois T. *Ruth*. San Francisco: Harper & Row, 1981.

Homes, Urban T. *A History Of Christian Spirituality*. New York: Seabury, 1980.

Houghton, Frank. *Quiet Time*. Downers Grove: InterVarsity, 1976.

Hummel, Charles. *Tyranny Of The Urgent*. Downers Grove: InterVarsity, 1967.

Hunter, W. Bingham. *The God Who Hears*. Downers Grove: InterVarsity, 1986.

Hybels, Lynne. *The Joy of Personal Worship*. Wheaton: Victor, 1984.

Jensen, Irving L. *Enjoy Your Bible*. Chicago: Moody, 1969.

_____ . *How To Profit From Bible Reading*. Chicago: Moody, 1985.

Jenson, Ronald A. *Biblical Mediation*. Oakland, Calif.: ICBI Press, 1982.

Job, John B., ed. *How To Study The Bible*. Downers Grove: InterVarsity, 1972.

Job, Reuben, and Norman Shawchuck. *A Guide to Prayer For Ministers and Other Servants*. Nashville: Upper Room, 1983.

Johnson, Charles W. Jr. *Fasting, Longevity and Immortality*, Haddam, Conn.: Survival, 1978.

Jones, E. Stanley. *A Song of Assent*. Nashville: Abingdon, 1968.

Kelsey, Morton T. *Adventure Inward*. Minneapolis: Augsburg, 1980.

——————. *The Other Side of Silence*. New York: Paulist, 1976.

Kempis, Thomas à. *The Imitation of Christ*. Garden City, NY: Image, 1955.

Kevson, Charles W. *Come Clean!*. Wheaton: Victor, 1976.

Kirban, Salem. *How To Keep Healthy and Happy By Fasting*. Irvine, Calif.: Harvest Home, 1976.

Klug, Ronald. *How To Keep a Spiritual Diary*. Nashville: Nelson, 1982.

——————. *My Prayer Journal*. St. Louis: Concordia, 1983.

The Kneeling Christian. Grand Rapids: Zondervan, 1971.

LaHaye, Tim. *How To Study The Bible For Yourself*. Irvine, Calif.: Harvest Home, 1976.

Lane, George A. *Christian Spirituality*. Chicago: Argus, 1968.

Law, William. *A Serious Call To A Devout and Holy Life*. Philadelphia: Westminster, 1955.

——————. *Selections On The Interior Life*. Wallingford, PA.: Pendle Hill, 1962.

247

Lawrence, Brother. *The Practice Of The Presence of God.* Old Tappan, NJ: Spire, 1958.

Leech, Kenneth. *Soul Friend.* San Francisco: Harper & Row, 1977.

_____ . *True Prayer.* San Francisco: Harper & Row, 1980.

LeSourd, Leonard, and Catherine Marshall. *My Personal Prayer Diary.* Lincoln, VA: Chosen Books, 1979.

Lewis, C.S. *The Business of Heaven.* Walter Hopper, ed. New York: Harcourt Brace Jovanovich, 1984.

_____ . *The Chronicles of Narnia.* 7 vols. New York: Collier, 1970.

_____ . *The Joyful Christian.* New York: Macmillan, 1977.

_____ . *The Screwtape Letters.* New York: Macmillan, 1961.

_____ . *The Visionary Christian*, Chad Walsh, ed. New York: Macmillan, 1981.

Lloyd-Jones, Dr. D. Martyn. *Preaching and Preachers.* Grand Rapids: Zondervan, 1971.

Luthi, Walter, and Edward Thurneysen. *Preaching, Confession, The Lord's Supper.* Richmond, VA: John Knox, 1957.

MacArthur, John. *Confession of Sin.* Chicago: Moody, 1986.

_____ . *The Ultimate Priority.* Chicago: Moody, 1983.

MacDonald, Gordon. *Ordering Your Private World.* Nashville: Oliver Nelson, 1984.

_____ . *Restoring Your Spiritual Passion.* Nashville: Oliver Nelson, 1986.

MacMillan, John. *The Authority Of The Believer.* Harrisburg, PA: Christian Publications, 1980.

Mains, Karen and David. *The Godhunt*. Chicago: Cook, 1984.

Marshall, Catherine. *Christy*. New York: Avon Books, 1967.

Massey, James Earl. *Spiritual Discipline*. Grand Rapids: Zondervan, 1985.

McCormick, Thomas, and Sharon Fish. *Meditation*. Downers Grove: InterVarsity, 1983.

McGinn, Bernard, and Meyendorff, eds. *Christian Spirituality I and II*. New York: Crossroads, 1985.

Miller, Calvin. *The Singer*. Downers Grove: InterVarsity, 1975.

——————. *The Table Of Inwardness*. Downers Grove: InterVarsity, 1984.

Mitchell, Curtis G. *Praying Jesus' Way*. Old Tappan, NJ: Revell, 1977.

Moody, D.L. *Prevailing Prayer*. Chicago: Revell, 1884.

Morrison, Mary C. *The Journal and The Journey*. Swarthmore, PA.: Purdie Hill, 1982.

Muck, Terry. *Liberating The Leader's Prayer Life*. Waco: Word, 1985.

——————. "10 Questions About the Devotional Life." *Leadership 3* (Winter 1982): 30-39.

Muggeridge, Malcolm. *Something Beautiful For God*. Harper & Row, 1971.

Muller, George. *Autobiography Of George Muller, The Life of Trust*. Edited by Lincoln Wayland. Grand Rapids: Baker, 1981.

Murchison, Anne. *Praise and Worship*. Waco: Word, 1981.

Murray, Andrew. *Confession and Forgiveness*. Grand Rapids: Zondervan, 1984.

——————. *The Inner Life*. Grand Rapids: Zondervan, 1980.

_____. *The Prayer Life*. New York: Doran, n.d.

_____. *With Christ In The School Of Prayer*. Westwood, NJ: Revell, 1953.

Myers, Warren. Pray: *How To Be Effective In Prayer*. Colorado Springs: NavPress, 1983.

Myers, Warren & Ruth Myers. *Praise: A Door To God's Presence*. Colorado Springs: NavPress, 1987.

The Navigator Bible Studies Handbook. Colorado Springs: NavPress, 1974.

Nee, Watchman. *The Normal Christian Life*. Fort Washington, PA: Christian Literature Crusade, 1963.

_____. *The Spiritual Man*, Vols. 1-3. New York: Christian Fellowship, 1968.

Nouwen, Henri. *Clowning In Rome*. Garden City, NY: Image, 1979.

_____. *The Genesee Diary*. Garden City, NY: Doubleday, 1976.

_____. *Making All Things New*. San Francisco: Harper & Row, 1981.

_____. *With Open Hands*. Notre Dame, Ind.: Ave Maria, 1972.

_____. *The Wounded Healer*. Garden City, NY: Doubleday, 1972.

Oates, Wayne. *The Holy Spirit In Five Worlds*. New York: Association Press, 1968.

Orr, J. Edwin. *Full Surrender*. London: Marshall, Morgan & Scott, 1951.

Padwick, Constance E. *Henry Martyn*. Chicago: Moody, 1980.

Palmer, W. Robert. *How To Understand The Bible*. Joplin, MO: College Press, 1980.

Parker, Percy Livingstone, ed. *The Journal of John Wesley*. Chicago: Moody, n.d.

Peace, Richard. *Pilgrimage.* Grand Rapids: Baker, 1976.

Pierson, Arthur T. *George Muller of Bristol.* Old Tappan, NJ: Revell, 1971.

Pipkin, H. Wayne. *Christian Meditation, Its Art and Practice.* New York: Hawthorn, 1977.

Prince, Derek. *Shaping History Through Prayer and Fasting.* Old Tappan, NJ: Revell, 1973.

Pittenger, Norman. *Praying Today.* Grand Rapids: Eerdmans, 1974.

Ray, David. *The Art of Christian Meditation.* Wheaton: Tyndale House, 1977.

Richard, Cecil. *The Life of John Newton.* Grand Rapids: Baker, 1978.

Rogers, Eric N. *Fasting: The Phenomenon Of Self-Denial.* Nashville: Nelson, 1976.

Rumford, Douglas J. "Keeping A Personal Journal." *Leadership 3* (Winter 1982): 56-57.

Ryan, John K., trans. *The Confessions of St. Augustine.* Garden City, NY: Image, 1960.

Sanders, J. Oswald. *Prayer Power Unlimited.* Chicago: Moody, 1977.

_____ . *Spiritual Leadership.* Chicago: Moody, 1980.

Santa-Maria, Maria. *Growth Through Meditation and Journal Writing.* New York: Paulist, 1973.

Schaeffer, Francis A. *The Mark of the Christian.* Downers Grove: InterVarsity, 1970.

_____ . *True Spirituality.* Wheaton: Tyndale House, 1971.

Shepherd, J. Barrie. *Prayers From The Mount.* Philadelphia: Westminster, 1986.

Shoemaker, Helen Smith. *Prayer and Evangelism.* Waco: Word, 1967.

Simons, George F. *Keeping Your Personal Journal*. New York: Paulist, 1978.

Smith, David P. *Fasting: A Neglected Discipline*. Fort Washington, PA: Christian Literature Crusade, 1954.

Smith, Hannah Whitall. *The Christian's Secret Of A Happy Life*. Old Tappan, NJ: Revell, 1970.

Smith, Leslie R. *Four Keys To Prayer*. St. Louis: Bethany Press, 1962.

Sterk, Andrea, and Peter Scazzero. *Christian Disciplines*. Downers Grove: InterVarsity, 1985.

Stott, John R. *Confess Your Sins*. Philadelphia: Westminster, 1964.

Sweet, Albert. *How To Study The Bible*. Austin: Sweet, 1963.

Swindoll, Charles. *Dropping Your Guard*. Waco: Word, 1983.

_____ . *Growing Deep In The Christian Life*. Portland, OR: Multnomah, 1986.

_____ . *Growing Strong In The Seasons Of Life*. Portland, OR: Multnomah, 1983.

_____ . *Improving Your Serve*. Waco: Word, 1981.

_____ . *Living Above The Level Of Mediocrity*. Waco: Word, 1987.

_____ . *The Quest For Character*. Portland, OR: Multnomah, n.d.

_____ . *Strengthening Your Grip*. Waco: Word, 1982.

Taylor, Jack R. Prayer: *Life's Limitless Reach*. Nashville: Broadman, 1977.

ten Boom, Corrie. *The Hiding Place*. Old Tappan, NJ: Revell, 1974.

Thomas, G. Ernest. *Spiritual Life In The New Testament*. Westwood, NJ: Revell, 1955.

Thurman, Howard. *The Inward Journey*. New York: Harper & Brothers, 1961.

Tozer, A.W. *How To Be Filled With The Holy Spirit*. Harrisburg, PA: Christian Publications, n.d.

_____ . *Keys To The Deeper Life*. Grand Rapids: Zondervan, 1957.

_____ . *The Pursuit of God*. Camp Hill, PA: Christian Publications, 1982.

Trueblood, Elton, *The Incendiary Fellowship*. San Francisco: Harper & Row, 1967.

_____ . *The New Man For Our Times*. New York: Harper & Row, 1970.

Underhill, Evelyn. *Worship*. New York: Harper & Brothers, 1937.

Wallis, Arthur. *God's Chosen Fast*. Fort Washington, PA: Christian Literature Crusade, 1968.

Warr, Gene. *The Godly Man*. Oklahoma City: The Warr Foundation, 1975.

Wemp, C. Sumner. *How On Earth Can I Be Spiritual?*. Nashville: Nelson, 1978.

Wesley, John. *The Journal Of John Wesley*. Percy Livingstone Parker. ed. Chicago: Moody, n.d.

White, John. *Bible Study*. Downers Grove: InterVarsity, 1976.

_____ . *Prayer*. Downers Grove: InterVarsity, 1976.

Whitney, Donald S. *Spiritual Disciplines for the Christian Life*. Colorado Springs: NavPress, 1991.

Willard, Dallas. *The Spirit of the Disciplines*. San Francisco: Harper & Row, 1988.

Wood, A. Skevington. *The Burning Heart*. Minneapolis: Bethany Fellowship, 1967.

SELECTED BIBLIOGRAPHY ON DISCIPLINES BY DISCIPLINE

General

Augsburger, Myron. *Called to Maturity*. Scottsdale, PA: Herald Press, 1960.

Benson, Bob, and Michael W. Benson. *Disciplines For the Inner Life*. Waco, TX: Word, 1985.

Boice, James Montgomery. *Christ's Call to Discipleship*. Chicago: Moody, 1986.

Bonhoeffer, Dietrich. *The Cost of Discipleship*. New York: Macmillan, 1949.

Bridges, Jerry. *The Pursuit of Godliness*. Colorado Springs: NavPress, n.d.

_____ . *The Pursuit of Holiness*. Colorado Springs: NavPress, 1978.

Briscoe, D. Stuart. *Getting Into God*. Grand Rapids: Zondervan, 1975.

Bubeck, Mark I. The Adversary. Chicago: Moody, 1984.

de Foucauld, Charles. *Meditations Of A Hermit*. London: Burns & Oates, n.d.

Fenhagen, James C. *More Than Wanderers*. New York: Seabury, 1978.

Ferré, Nels. *Strengthening The Spiritual Life*. New York: Harper & Brothers, 1951.

Foster, Richard J. *Celebration of Discipline*. San Francisco: Harper & Row, 1978.

Gritter, George. *The Quest For Holiness*. Grand Rapids: Eerdmans, 1955.

Growing Strong in God's Family. Colorado Springs: Nav-Press, 1987.

Gunsaulus, Frank W. *The Minister and Spiritual Life*. New York: Revell, 1911.

Holmes, Urban T. *A History of Christian Spirituality*. New York: Seabury, 1980.

Kelsey, Morton, T. *Adventure Inward*. Minneapolis: Augsburg, 1980.

Lane, George A. *Christian Spirituality*. Chicago: Argus, 1968.

Law, William. *A Serious Call To A Devout and Holy Life*. Philadelphia: Westminster, 1955.

MacDonald, Gordon. *Ordering Your Private World*. Nashville: Oliver Nelson, 1984.

_____. *Restoring Your Spiritual Passion*. Nashville: Oliver Nelson, 1986.

MacMillan, John, *The Authority Of The Believer*. Harrisburg, PA: Christian Publications, 1980.

Massey, James Earl. *Spiritual Discipline*. Grand Rapids: Zondervan, 1985.

McGinn, Bernard, and Meyendorff, eds. *Christian Spirituality I and II*. New York: Crossroads, 1985.

Miller, Calvin. *The Table of Inwardness*. Downers Grove: InterVarsity, 1984.

Murray, Andrew. *The Inner Life*. Grand Rapids: Zondervan, 1980.

Nee, Watchman. *The Normal Christian Life*. Fort Washington, PA: Christian Literature Crusade, 1963.

_____. *The Spiritual Man*, Vols. 1-3. New York: Christian Fellowship, 1968.

Nouwen, Henri. *The Wounded Healer*. Garden City, NY: Doubleday, 1972.

Oates, Wayne. *The Holy Spirit in Five Worlds*. New York: Association Press, 1968.

Peace, Richard. *Pilgrimage*. Grand Rapids: Baker, 1976.

Sanders, J. Oswald. *Spiritual Leadership*. Chicago: Moody, 1980.

Schaeffer, Francis A. *The Mark of the Christian*. Downers Grove: InterVarsity, 1970.

_____. *True Spirituality*. Wheaton: Tyndale House, 1971.

Smith, Hannah Whitall. *The Christian's Secret Of A Happy Life*. Old Tappan, NJ: Revell, 1970.

Sterk, Andrea, and Peter Scazzero. *Christian Disciplines*. Downers Grove: InterVarsity, 1985.

Thomas, G. Ernest. *Spiritual Life In The New Testament*. Westwood, NJ: Revell, 1955.

Thurman, Howard. *The Inward Journey*. New York: Harper & Brothers, 1961.

Tozer, A.W. *How To Be Filled With The Holy Spirit*. Harrisburg, PA: Christian Publications, n.d.

_____. *Keys To The Deeper Life*. Grand Rapids: Zondervan, 1957.

_____. *The Pursuit of God*. Camp Hill, PA: Christian Publications, 1982.

Trueblood, Elton. *The New Man For Our Times*. New York: Harper & Row, 1970.

Wemp, C. Sumner. *How On Earth Can I Be Spiritual?*. Nashville: Nelson, 1978.

Whitney, Donald S. *Spiritual Disciplines for the Christian Life*. Colorado Springs: NavPress, 1991.

Willard, Dallas. *The Spirit of the Disciplines*. San Francisco: Harper & Row, 1988.

Prayer

Augsburger, Myron. *Called To Maturity.* Scottsdale, PA: Herald Press, 1960.

Belden, Albert. *The Practice Of Prayer.* New York: Harper & Brothers, n.d.

Bennett, Arthur, ed. *Valley Of Vision.* Edinburgh: Banner of Truth, 1975.

Bewes, Richard. *Talking About Prayer.* Downers Grove: InterVarsity, 1979.

Bisagno, John. *The Power Of Positive Praying.* Grand Rapids: Zondervan, 1965.

Blanchard, Charles A. *Getting Things From God.* Chicago: Bible Institute Colportage Assoc., 1915.

Bloom, Anthony. *Beginning To Pray.* New York: Paulist, 1970.

_____. *Courage To Pray.* New York: Paulist, 1973.

_____. *God & Man.* New York: Paulist, 1971.

_____. *Living Prayer.* London: Libra, 1966.

Bounds, Edward M. *The Essentials Of Prayer.* New York: Revell, 1925.

_____. *The Necessity Of Prayer.* Grand Rapids: Baker, 1978.

_____. *The Possibilites Of Prayer.* Grand Rapids: Baker, 1979.

_____. *Power Through Prayer.* Grand Rapids: Zondervan, 1961.

_____. *Prayer And The Praying Man.* New York: Doran, 1921.

_____. *Purpose In Prayer.* Chicago: Moody, n.d.

_____. *The Reality Of Prayer.* Chicago: Moody, 1980.

_____. *A Treasury Of Prayer.* Minneapolis: Bethany Fellowship, 1961.

_____ . *The Weapon Of Prayer*. New York: Revell, 1931.

Bubeck, Mark I. *The Adversary*. Chicago: Moody, 1984.

Casteel, John L. *Rediscovering Prayer*. New York: Association Press, 1955.

Eastman, Dick. *The Hour That Changes The World*. Grand Rapids: Baker, 1978.

_____ . *No Easy Road*. Grand Rapids: Baker, 1971.

Edward, Jonathan. *Life And Diary of David Brainerd*. New Haven, Conn.: Yale University Press, 1984.

Elliff, Thomas D. *Praying For Others*. Nashville: Broadman, 1979.

Fosdick, Harry Emerson. *The Meaning of Prayer*. Nashville: Abingdon, 1949.

Foster, Richard J. *Celebration Of Discipline*. San Francisco: Harper & Row, 1978.

_____ . *Finding the Heart's True Home*. San Francisco: Harper, 1992.

God's Power Through Prayer. Houston: Countryman Pub., n.d.

Gordon, S.D. *Quiet Talks On How To Pray*. New York: Revell, 1929.

Hunter, W. Bingham. *The God Who Hears*. Downers Grove: InterVarsity, 1986.

The Kneeling Christian. Grand Rapids: Zondervan, 1971.

Leech, Kenneth. *Soul Friend*. San Francisco: Harper & Row, 1977.

_____ . *True Prayer*. San Francisco: Harper & Row, 1980.

Lloyd-Jones, Dr. D. Martyn. *Preaching and Preachers*. Grand Rapids: Zondervan, 1971.

Massey, James Earl. *Spiritual Discipline*. Grand Rapids: Zondervan, 1985.

Mitchell, Curtis G. *Praying Jesus' Way*. Old Tappan, NJ: Revell, 1977.

Moody, D.L. *Prevailing Prayer*. Chicago: Revell, 1884.

Muck, Terry, *Liberating The Leader's Prayer Life*. Waco: Word, 1985.

Muller, George. *Autobiography Of George Muller, The Life of Trust*. Edited by Lincoln Wayland. Grand Rapids: Baker, 1981.

Murray, Andrew. *The Prayer Life*. New York: Doran, n.d.

_____. *With Christ In The School Of Prayer*. Westwood, NJ: Revell, 1953.

Myers, Warren. Pray: *How To Be Effective In Prayer*. Colorado Springs: NavPress, 1983.

Nouwen, Henri. *Clowning In Rome*. Garden City, NY: Image, 1979.

_____. *With Open Hands*. Notre Dame, Ind.: Ave Maria, 1972.

Pittenger, Norman. *Praying Today*. Grand Rapids: Eerdmans, 1974.

Sanders, J. Oswald. *Prayer Power Unlimited*. Chicago: Moody, 1977.

Shepherd, J. Barrie. *Prayers From The Mount*. Philadelphia: Westminster, 1986.

Shoemaker, Helen Smith. *Prayer And Evangelism*. Waco: Word, 1974.

Smith, Leslie R. *Four Keys To Prayer*. St. Louis: Bethany Press, 1962.

Taylor, Jack R. *Prayer: Life's Limitless Reach*. Nashville: Broadman, 1977.

White, John. *Prayer*. Downers Grove: InterVarsity, 1976.

Confession

Augsburger, Myron. *Called To Maturity*. Scottsdale, PA: Herald Press, 1960.

Bowman, George William III. *The Dynamics Of Confession*. Richmond, VA: John Knox, n.d.

Foster, Richard J. *Celebration Of Discipline*. San Francisco: Harper & Row, 1978.

Keyson, Charles W. *Come Clean!*. Wheaton: Victor, 1976.

Luthi, Walter, and Edward Thurneysen. *Preaching, Confession, The Lord's Supper*. Richmond, VA: John Knox, 1957.

MacArthur, John. *Confession of Sin*. Chicago: Moody, 1986.

Moody, D.L. *Prevailing Prayer*. Chicago: Revell, 1884.

Murray, Andrew. *Confession and Forgiveness*. Grand Rapids: Zondervan, 1984.

Orr, J. Edwin. *Full Surrender*. London: Marshall, Morgan & Scott, 1951.

Stott, John R. *Confess Your Sins*. Philadelphia: Westminster, 1964.

Bible Study

Adeney, Carol, ed. *This Morning With God*. Downers Grove: InterVarsity, 1978.

Bonhoeffer, Dietrich. *Meditating On The Word*. Cambridge, MA: Cowley, 1986.

Conyers, A.J. *How To Read The Bible*. Downers Grove: InterVarsity, 1986.

Cooper, Clay. "Four Reasons Why We Need The Bible." *Christian Standard*, 15 October 1966, 7-8.

Fee, Gordon, and Douglas Stuart. *How To Read The Bible For All It's Worth*. Grand Rapids: Zondervan, 1982.

Foster, Lewis. *Selecting A Translation Of The Bible*. Cincinnati: Standard, 1983.

Foster, Richard J. *Celebration Of Discipline*. San Francisco: Harper & Row, 1978.

Halley, Henry H. *Bible Handbook*. Grand Rapids: Zondervan, 1962.

Hathaway, Homer. "Who Reads the Bible Today?" *Christian Standard*. 4 October 1970, 9-10.

Jensen, Irving L. *Enjoy Your Bible*. Chicago: Moody, 1969.
_____. *How To Profit From Bible Reading*. Chicago: Moody, 1985.

Job, John B., ed. *How To Study The Bible*. Downers Grove: InterVarsity, 1972.

LaHaye, Tim. *How To Study The Bible For Yourself*. Irvine, Calif.: Harvest Home, 1976.

The Navigator Bible Studies Handbook. Colorado Springs: NavPress, 1974.

Palmer, W. Robert. *How To Understand The Bible*. Joplin, MO: College Press, 1980.

Sweet, Albert. *How To Study The Bible*. Austin: Sweet, 1963.

White, John. *Bible Study*. Downers Grove: InterVarsity, 1976.

Reading

Allison, Joseph O. *The Devotional Resource Guide*. Nashville: Nelson, 1986.

Augustine. *Confessions*. Translated by Edward Pusey. New York: Macmillan, 1961.

Bainton, Roland H. *Here I Stand*. Nashville: Abingdon, 1950.

Bonhoeffer, Dietrich. *The Cost Of Discipleship*. New York: Macmillan, 1949.

_____ . *Life Together*. New York: Harper & Row, 1954.

_____ . *The Martyred Christian*. Joan Winmill Brown, ed. New York: Macmillan, 1983.

Brainerd, David. *The Life Of David Brainerd*. Grand Rapids: Baker, 1978.

Bunyan, John. *The Pilgrim's Progress*. Old Tappan, NJ: Revell, 1965.

Colson, Charles W. *Born Again*. Falls Church, VA: Conservative Press, 1976.

Conwell, Russell N. *Acres Of Diamonds*. Old Tappan, NJ: Revell, 1975.

de Sales, Francis. *Introdution To A Devout Life*. New York: World Publishing, 1952.

Elliot, Elizabeth. *Through Gates Of Splendor*. New York: Harper & Row, 1958.

Foster, Richard J. *Celebration Of Discipline*. San Francisco: Harper & Row, 1978.

Henderson, Lois T. *Ruth*. San Francisco: Harper & Row, 1981.

Kempis, Thomas à. *The Imitation of Christ*. Garden City, NY: Image, 1955.

Law, William. *A Serious Call To A Devout and Holy Life*. Philadelphia: Westminster, 1955.

Lawrence, Brother. *The Practice Of The Presence of God*. Old Tappan, NJ: Spire, 1958.

Lewis, C.S. *The Business of Heaven*. Walter Hooper, ed. New York: Harcourt Brace Jovanovich, 1984.

_____ . *The Chronicles of Narnia*. 7 vols. New York: Collier, 1970.

_____ . *The Joyful Christian*. New York: Macmillan, 1977.

_____ . *The Screwtape Letters*. New York: Macmillan, 1961.

_____ . *The Visionary Christian*. Chad Walsh, ed. New York: Macmillan, 1981.

Marshall, Catherine. *Christy*. New York: Avon Books, 1967.

Miller, Calvin. *The Singer*. Downers Grove: InterVarsity, 1975.

Padwick, Constance E. *Henry Martyn*. Chicago: Moody, 1980.

Pierson, Arthur T. *George Muller of Bristol*. Old Tappan, NJ: Revell, 1971.

Richard, Cecil. *The Life of John Newton*. Grand Rapids: Baker, 1978.

Ryan, John K., trans. *The Confessions of St. Augustine*. Garden City, NY: Image, 1960.

Swindoll, Charles. *Dropping Your Guard*. Waco: Word, 1983.

_____ . *Living Above The Level Of Mediocrity*. Waco: Word, 1987.

_____ . *Strengthening Your Grip*. Waco: Word, 1982.

ten Boom, Corrie. *The Hiding Place*. Old Tappan, NJ: Revell, 1974.

Wood, A. Skevington. *The Burning Heart*. Minneapolis: Bethany Fellowship, 1967.

Journaling

Brainerd, David. *The Life Of David Brainerd*. Grand Rapids: Baker, 1978.

Cargas, Harry J., and Roger Radley. *Keeping A Spiritual Journal*. Garden City, NJ: Doubleday, 1981.

Fenhagen, James C. *More Than Wanderers.* New York: Seabury, 1978.

Klug, Ronald. *How To Keep a Spiritual Diary.* Nashville: Nelson, 1982.

──────── . *My Prayer Journal.* St. Louis: Concordia, 1983.

LeSourd, Leonard, and Catherine Marshall. *My Personal Prayer Diary.* Lincoln, VA: Chosen Books, 1979.

Mains, Karen and David. *The Godhunt.* Chicago: Cook, 1984.

Morrison, Mary C. *The Journal and The Journey.* Swarthmore, PA.: Purdle Hill, 1982.

Parker, Percy Livingstone, ed. *The Journal of John Wesley.* Chicago: Moody, n.d.

Rumford, Douglas J. "Keeping A Personal Journal." *Leadership 3* (Winter 1982): 56-57.

Santa-Maria, Maria. *Growth Through Meditation & Journal Writing.* New York: Paulist, 1973.

Simons, George F. *Keeping Your Personal Journal.* New York: Paulist, 1978.

Meditation/Solitude

Andrews, C.F. *Christ In The Silence.* New York: Abingdon, 1933.

Belden, Albert. *The Practice Of Prayer.* New York: Harper & Brothers, n.d.

Bloom, Anthony. *Living Prayer.* London: Libra, 1966.

Bonhoeffer, Dietrich. *Meditating On The Word.* Cambridge, MA: Cowley, 1986.

Clowney, Edmund P. *Christian Meditation.* Nutley, NJ: Craig Press, 1979.

Downing, Jim. *Meditation*. Colorado Springs: NavPress, 1976.

Finley, James. *The Awakening Call*. Notre Dame, Ind.: Ave Maria Press, n.d.

Fleming, Jean. *Between Walden And The Whirlwind*. Colorado Springs: NavPress, n.d.

Foster, Richard J. *Celebration Of Discipline*. San Francisco: Harper & Row, 1978.

_____ . *Meditative Prayer*. Downers Grove: InterVarsity, 1983.

Hanson, Bradley. *The Call of Silence*. Minneapolis: Augsburg, 1980.

Hummel, Charles. *Tyranny Of The Urgent*. Downers Grove: InterVarsity, 1967.

Jenson, Ronald A. *Biblical Meditation*. Oakland, Calif.: ICBI Press, 1982.

Kelsey, Morton T. *The Other Side of Silence*. New York: Paulist, 1976.

McCormick, Thomas, and Sharon Fish. *Meditation*. Downers Grove: InterVarsity, 1983.

Nouwen, Henri. *Clowning In Rome*. Garden City, NY: Image, 1979.

_____ . *The Genesee Diary*. Garden City, NY: Doubleday, 1976.

_____ . *Making All Things New*. San Francisco: Harper & Row, 1981.

Pipkin, H. Wayne. *Christian Meditation, Its Art and Practice*. New York: Hawthorn, 1977.

Ray, David. *The Art of Christian Meditation*. Wheaton: Tyndale House, 1977.

Santa-Maria, Maria. *Growth Through Meditation and Journal Writing*. New York: Paulist, 1973.

Smith, Leslie R. *Four Keys To Prayer.* St. Louis: Bethany Press, 1962.

Devotional Life

Benson, Bob, and Michael W. Benson. *Disciplines For The Inner Life.* Waco, TX: Word, 1985.

Chambers, Oswald. *My Utmost For His Highest.* New York: Dodd, Mead, & Co., n.d.

Clark, Kelly James. *Quiet Times For Christian Growth.* Downers Grove: InterVarsity, 1979.

Claydon, Graham. *Time With God.* Grand Rapids: Zondervan, 1979.

Conyers, A.J. *How To Read The Bible.* Downers Grove: InterVarsity, 1986.

Conwell, Russell N. *Acres Of Diamonds.* Old Tappan, NJ: Revell, 1975.

Cowman, Mrs. Charles E. *Streams In The Desert.* Grand Rapids: Zondervan, 1965.

DeWelt, Don. *Prayer Time, A Guide For Personal Worship.* Joplin, MO: College Press, 1982.

Dunham, Maxie. *The Workbook On Spiritual Disciplines.* Nashville: Upper Room, 1984.

Ferré, Nels. *Strengthening The Spiritual Life.* New York: Harper & Brothers, 1951.

Foster, Richard J., and Henri Nouwen. "Hearing God's Voice and . . . : Interview with Richard J. Foster and Henri Nouwen," interview by Terry Muck, Harold Myra, and Roy Coffman, *Leadership 3* (Winter 1982): 16-29.

Foster, Robert D. *Seven Minutes With God.* Colorado Springs: NavPress, n.d.

Halverson, Richard C. *No Greater Power*. Portland, OR: Multnomah, 1986.

Houghton, Frank. *Quiet Time*. Downers Grove: InterVarsity, 1976.

Job, Reuben, and Norman Shawchuck. *A Guide to Prayer For Ministers and Other Servants*. Nashville: Upper Room, 1983.

Muck, Terry. "10 Questions About the Devotional Life." *Leadership 3* (Winter 1982): 30-39.

Swindoll, Charles. *Growing Deep In The Christian Life*. Portland, OR: Multnomah, 1986.

_____ . *Growing Strong In The Seasons Of Life*. Portland, OR: Multnomah, 1983.

_____ . *The Quest For Character*. Portland, OR: Multnomah, n.d.

Warr, Gene. *The Godly Man*. Oklahoma City: The Warr Foundation, 1975.

Fasting

Anderson, Andy. *Fasting Changed My Life*. Nashville: Broadman, n.d.

Beall, James Lee. *The Adventure Of Fasting*. Old Tappan, NJ: Revell, 1974.

DeWelt, Don. *Prayer and Fasting*. Joplin, MO: Ozark Bible College, n.d. Typewritten.

Falwell, Jerry. *Fasting*. Wheaton: Tyndale House, 1981.

Foster, Richard J. *Celebration Of Discipline*. San Francisco: Harper & Row, 1978.

_____ . "Fasting: Twentieth Century Style." *Theological Students Fellowship Bulletin* (November-December 1983): 14-16.

Johnson, Charles W. Jr. *Fasting, Longevity and Immortality*. Haddam, Conn.: Survival, 1978.

Kirban, Salem. *How To Keep Healthy and Happy By Fasting*. Irvine, Calif.: Harvest Home, 1976.

Massey, James Earl. *Spiritual Discipline*. Grand Rapids: Zondervan, 1985.

Prince, Derek. *Shaping History Through Prayer And Fasting*. Old Tappan, NJ: Revell, 1973.

Rogers, Eric N. *Fasting: The Phenomenon Of Self-Denial*. Nashville: Nelson, 1976.

Smith, David R. *Fasting: A Neglected Discipline*. Fort Washington, PA: Christian Literature Crusade, 1954.

Wallis, Arthur. *God's Chosen Fast*. Fort Washington, PA: Christian Literature Crusade, 1968.

Wemp, C. Sumner. *How On Earth Can I Be Spiritual?* Nashville: Nelson, 1978.

Personal Worship

DeWelt, Don. *Personal Worship* (in seven volumes). Joplin: College Press, 1988-1990.

_____ . *Sweet Hour of Prayer*. Joplin: College Press, 1984.

Foster, Richard J. *Celebration Of Discipline*. San Francisco: Harper & Row, 1978.

Hybels, Lynne. *The Joy of Personal Worship*. Wheaton: Victor, 1984.

MacArthur, John. *The Ultimate Priority*. Chicago: Moody, 1983.

Massey, James Earl. *Spiritual Discipline*. Grand Rapids: Zondervan, 1985.

Murchison, Anne. *Praise and Worship*. Waco: Word, 1981.

Myers, Warren & Ruth Myers. *Praise: A Door To God's Presence*. Colorado Springs: NavPress, 1987.

Underhill, Evelyn. *Worship*. New York: Harper & Brothers, 1937.

Ministry

Bernardin, Joseph. *The Ministry Of Service*. Collegeville, MN: Liturgical Press, 1985.

Fenhagen, James C. *More Than Wanderers*. New York: Seabury, 1978.

Foster, Richard J. *Celebration Of Discipline*. San Francisco: Harper & Row, 1978.

Gordon, S.D. *Quiet Talks On Service*. New York: Revell, 1906.

Muggeridge, Malcolm. *Something Beautiful For God*. Harper & Row, 1971.

Shoemaker, Helen Smith. *Prayer And Evangelism*. Waco: Word, 1967.

Swindoll, Charles. *Improving Your Serve*. Waco: Word, 1981.

Trueblood, Elton. *The Incendiary Fellowship*. San Francisco: Harper & Row, 1967.

About the Author

John Caldwell is Senior Minister of the Kingsway Christian Church in the Indianapolis suburb of Avon, Indiana, where he has served since June of 1974.

John received his B.Th. and M.Min. from Ozark Christian College, his M.Div. from Cincinnati Christian Seminary, and D.Min. from Trinity Evangelical Divinity School. John has served on the adjunct faculty of Cincinnati Bible Seminary since 1985. He has authored several books, among which is *Top Priority: Building an Evangelistic Church.*

Dr. Caldwell has conducted more than 190 crusades in 20 states as well as Australia, New Zealand, Haiti, Jamaica, India, and Zimbabwe. John was named as President of the North American Christian Convention in Dallas, Texas in 1996. He has served on the Continuation Committees for both the National Missionary and Indiana Christian Conventions. John has also served as President of the Indiana State Men's Fellowship and has been listed in *Who's Who in Religion.*

Kingsway Christian Church has been one of the fastest growing churches in Indiana, growing to an average of nearly 1600 with a record attendance of 2391. Kingsway recently completed its fifth building program.

John and his wife, Jan, have a son, Shan, and daughter, Jennifer, who are active in service to the Lord.